AMBIANCE / ALMOST FREE PLAYSCRIPTS 1

HOMOSEXUAL ACTS

Five short Plays from The Gay Season at The Almost Free Theatre

Edited by Ed Berman

Inter-Action Inprint, 14 Talacre Road London NW5 3PE 1975

Made and printed in Great Britain by
Hill & Garwood Printing Limited, Wembley.

CONTENTS

INTRODUCTION

GRIM AND GAY
or
IT'S NOT JUST A TRIP, YOU KNOW

The Almost Free is a name chosen for literal reasons: you pay what you feel you can afford. But more important than the box office policy is the artistic policy: we produce what we feel will lead to the action lip of 'liberation'

Trendy words deserve to be strait-jacketed and "liberation" is surely one of the most manic inmates of our current vocabulary. Plays and theatres cannot liberate. They might at best inspire people to think or to bring thinkers to the brink of action.

The theatre can almost do a direct job with reality, but never quite. No matter how environmental the piece, no matter how documentary the material, no matter how communal the cast and audience, the fact is that Theatre treats with a representation, an illusion, a mirror—but not the thing itself. It is almost real and therefore almost free and thus almost liberating.

One aspect of our approach to Social Theatre brings us a step closer to Almost Free. Whenever we produce a season based on a social issue, we try to find a group of people who are themselves intimately involved in the issue. We try to find them not as they would find themselves, as an audience, but as co-producers. The very people who are the subject matter of Social Theatre themselves must find a platform and control the production of the material. They must learn to play the administration, management, publicity and technical roles. It is not sufficient and perhaps not even necessary for them exclusively to be the actors, writers and directors.

A Black theatre in presenting plays will often need White actors. A homosexual theatre will occasionally use non-gay writers, actors and actresses. A women's theatre may sometimes require actors.

Purity is never the question because there is no touchstone, no single standard for social purity. Control over the many aspects of theatre production machinery is the key to a liberating self-determined voice in

Social Theatre. Ideas are free; but action is costly; and buildings, wages and greasepaint are expensive.

In order to give an opportunity to a group who felt oppressed and wanted to acquire the tools to run a theatre machine, we went out to find some individuals with this desire. The opportunity might itself galvanize them into a group. After several open meetings with dozens of people, a group began to form to take advantage of the opportunity of co-producing a season with Inter-Action on the theme of homo-sexuality. In order for them to become independent as a gay theatre group it was necessary for them to learn all aspects of the business including the behind-the-scenes jobs that many had never been in contact with before.
If you can't screw the nuts and bolts, you can't run your own machine.

They named themselves The Gay Sweatshop and here, for reasons of self-expression, I let Roger Baker take over the story:

"Why a *gay* theatre group? This is a question that has been asked many times since the existence of Gay Sweatshop became known. The idea that homosexuals might identify themselves and concentrate energy in one particular area is still greeted with bewilderment, apprehension and, sometimes, scorn. The very reality of such reactions is, in fact, an answer to the question.

"The existence of homosexuals is something that society generally prefers not to know about. Aware of this, homosexuals collude and continue to perform their perfect disappearing act. This collusion, which means that the homosexual denies the reality of self, is oppression. It operates insidiously, weaving through the texture of the life of every gay woman and man.

"Since 1970, the gay movement in this country has, under its various banners, been fighting this oppression. One result has been a move for gay members of specific professions to get together, especially in those professions that are conventionally hostile to homosexuality.

"Though groups for gay policemen, gay priests and gay psychiatrists have yet to emerge in this country, there are now active groups of gay librarians, gay civil servants, gay teachers, gay journalists and gay social workers. The significance of this list is that the necessity to act has arisen from within the ranks of those already employed. Also these are power-wielding professions; one way or another, the members of these professions can and do operate authority and influence over others. Part of their authoritarian parcel is an assertion of the status quo which means the supremacy of men, the inferiority of women and the rejection of gays. Homosexuals from within the ranks are contesting these assumptions.

"The theatre presents a different kind of situation. No sense of gay identification has emerged from the theatre, be it mainstream, fringe or experimental. Yet, traditionally, the theatre is popularly supposed to employ a higher percentage of homosexuals than any other profession. Members of Gay Sweatshop who have approached professional actors and directors have met with responses ranging from guarded interest to downright terror.

"This suggests that gay oppression in the theatre is very heavy. It seems that, as in many other areas of life, in the theatre the homosexual is tolerated so long as he keeps it 'private'; but for him or her to take a positive attitude towards it will be met with high displeasure. Yet, in its end product—that is, what the public pay to see—the theatre, be it stage, screen, radio or television, projects a fairly savage attitude towards homosexuals.

"The entertainment industry uses its enormous power to reinforce the stereotyped response to the homosexual as being either a huge joke, or an object of disgust and pity. Such attitudes have been implicit in a number of shows seen in London since 1972, and to which audiences have flocked, notably 'SECTION 9', 'THE ROCKY HORROR SHOW' and 'OFF THE PEG'. Examples could be multiplied, of course, from the effeminate man as a stock comic prop in comedy through to the self-styled 'liberation' of 'LET MY PEOPLE COME'. Here, male homosexuals are treated with gooey sentiment (objects of pity), while female homosexuals are shown making physical love (objects for male heterosexual titillation).

"As Andrew Hodges and David Hutter point out in their book 'WITH DOWNCAST GAYS': 'Far from feeling resentment at the commercialised mockery of their lives, homosexuals seem positively to revel in it. More than this, as comedians, script-

writers, novelists and publishers, they *create* it.' In the list of
shows just mentioned, and in all those similar, there must have
been homosexuals involved, who perhaps helped to direct, act,
light, choreograph and paint them. Such collusion in putting down
gay men and women, themselves therefore, is the ultimate in
self-oppression.

"Audiences are invited to deride gays. But audiences include
homosexuals as well, and they too will willingly enter into the
complicity and go armoured to withstand the barbs and grotesque
parodies of themselves. No murmer of protest is heard.

"Gay Sweatshop has been created to suggest an alternative to all
this. During the last few years some efforts have been made to
relate gay activism and the theatre, notably with a street theatre
group formed from out of the Gay Liberation Front. But
enthusiasm, stamina and personnel tend to evaporate which is why
we called our outfit a Sweatshop—to indicate, if nothing else, it
would be hard work.

"It seemed that, to get such a project moving, a certain goal was
needed. This came early last year when Ed Berman of Inter-Action
sent out a call asking whether it was possible to form a gay theatre
group, along the lines of the Women's Theatre Group and
Women's Company that Inter-Action had previously encouraged
through the 'Women's Theatre Season'.

"The individuals that came along were all connected with the
theatre—as writers, technicians, film-makers and so on—though
none were employed full-time in any theatre. Everyone also
represented different viewpoints on gay politics. Gay Sweatshop
would not claim therefore to represent the views of all gay people,
but simply the views we arrived at ourselves."

There were many areas to be sorted out between Inter-Action and the
Gay Sweatshop in order for the season to fulfil its ambitions.
Ultimately the season had to be a success in theatrical terms because
no-one in Social Theatre should expect points to be given for being on
the side of the angels. Social Theatre productions must not be self-
indulgent because of a holier-than-thou sub-text. In the Theatre, as
much as in any other art form, it's what's up/out front that counts. In

theory Social Theatre productions will be all the more pointed, incisive and poignant because they are self-expressive. In practice, this will only be true if the theatre skills are as good or better than the bourgeois theatre surrounding us.

Naturally conflicts occur within groups of principle-bearing people. A group which is a laminate of theatre people and political activists will feel the stress from one side or the other regularly as each group comes at the mutual goal from a different vantage point. Often the group will split up along the lines of Principles - First-Damn-The-Theatre v. Theatre-Standards-Must-Not-Be-Sacrificed-To-Boring-Preachers.

This happened to some degree with the Gay Sweatshop although ultimately Inter-Action had the final say in which plays were produced (after an initial vetting by the Sweatshop members).

At the beginning of the season there was a hard line in evidence that all plays should be new British plays—none from America would be allowed. Further, all actors, writers, directors, stage crew and non-Inter-Action management were to be gay. These lines were altered by the middle of the season as witnessed by the inclusion of the Robert Patrick plays.

The arguments that raged brought crises to the Sweatshop; members resigned or lost interest as the differences between each particular viewer and the central democratically decided image crystallized.

The Gay Sweatshop continued in operation as an independent theatre production company after the Almost Free Homosexual Acts season in 1975. They had no regular source of income from the theatre, no premises and no equipment. They did have energetic talented committed people, however. But will these be enough to survive in a culture where the 'right ideas' are not necessarily sufficient to allow a minority group to overcome prejudice? The willingness and ability to express a self are not necessarily sufficient to obtain a platform.

When times are grim do you simply allow reaction to overtake whatever gains have been made in civilizing one's native land? Does one out-front theatre group stand a chance against the ingrained prejudice of centuries? Yes, if it allies itself with other groups and avoids preaching to the converted.

For more dramatic answers to these and other ambitious questions, tune in to your own Social Theatre for the next exciting chapter in The Story Of How Theatre Was Almost Free. In any case, artists must stop being so arrogant as to think that they are completely free of social responsibility in their work.

We feel that people can use Theatre to go further than Shaftesbury Avenue and Broadway (on, off, or off-off). It's not just a trip, you know.

Ed Berman
Artistic Director
Inter-Action Productions

London, 1975

'ONE PERSON'
by Robert Patrick

The first performance in the United Kingdom of 'One Person' was at
The Ambiance Lunch-Hour Theatre Club (situated at Inter-Action's
Almost Free Theatre, Rupert Street, London W1) on Monday, 12th
May, 1975, with:

    Michael Deacon

An Inter-Action Production directed by Stewart Trotter.

Approximate playing time: 35 minutes

The play takes place on the bare stage of the theatre where it is performed. One wooden chair is needed. The only character is the AUTHOR. HE is referred to in the script as long-haired and barefoot, but this is not mandatory. HE will pantomime all props, scenery and costume changes throughout the piece. This includes the nude scenes, for which HE must not actually remove any clothing. Where music is referred to in the script, actual music may be used, but it will be all the better if the AUTHOR can simply move as if it were there. Although some of the other characters' lines are included here to help the AUTHOR in his responses, they are not to be heard. Good luck.

> In the darkness, we hear the AUTHOR singing some very sad love song but with style and humour. I suggest "That's When Your Heartaches Begin," in imitation of Elvis Presley. A single spotlight then reveals the AUTHOR. HE searches among the audience and then smiles brightly.

AUTHOR: Hello. I'm happy to see you out there among the audience. Oh, I'm happy to see the audience, too, of course. Hi, audience! Hello, audience! Mmmmmmmmmm, I love you, do your audience thing—

> HE poses, smiles, waves and blows kisses like a "showbiz" personality, then subsides and becomes serious and tender.

I'm very sorry, audience, to misuse my powers of public assembly, granted me by the nether gods, to drag you all down here under false pretenses. I know you thought you were going to see one of my usual fun-for-all plays, but this one—

> HE finds once again the face in the audience that made him smile.

—this one is for you.

> HE makes the gesture which will mark his meetings with that person, both palms held out before him as if to meet another's hands.

I hope that doesn't embarrass you, but I had to see you again. I had to have one more chance to talk with you in private, and this is as private as we seem to be able to get. When we are in private, we don't seem to be able to talk, not about what we need to talk about, we don't seem to be able to touch (Palm gesture) as we used to. We always have something in our hands, a cigarette or a drink—(Takes them from the air) and we can't touch.

> HE reaches out, realizes HE holds "drink" and "cigarette," and carefully places them out of the way in the air.

It's like it was back before we ever touched, before we ever met. Can you remember? I was one person, and you were one person, and then we—we were one person, and then—and then what? What happened? We were ONE PERSON—and that person—I guess—became lonely.

> HE sits, laughing, in the chair. HE is in a restaurant with his lover. HE extends his palms across the table, but the lover is reluctant to be touched in public.

Oh, all right, all right, you're right. You have this curious capacity for being able to remember that there are other people in the world. Look, see, I'll fill my hands up with—with toast and coffee. I've learned that the second rule of a love affair is that you don't touch when you're out in public.

> Lover asks: "What's the first rule?"

The first rule is: "Don't go out in public." What are the rules about touching knees under the table? Is that allowed?

> HE slides comically low to let their knees touch. The lover objects.

What do you mean, "people are watching?" Who's watching? (Turns to look) Oh, for heaven's sake, that's all right. I know them. That's Gene and Pablo. They're—well—together—like us. Come on, you should meet them anyway—you haven't met any of my friends. Please, come on. (Holds out hand, stands) No, take my hand, it's all right.

> They join hands and walk over to Gene and Pablo's table. AUTHOR assumes his bright, flashy public personality.

Gene, Pablo, hello angels, how in the world are you? You look fabulous. (Touches his hair) Yes, I'm letting it grow again. (To lover) I cut it last year for unrequited love—and that's exactly what I got for it. (To Gene) Yours looks marvellous, I've never seen it longer, you're becoming the Lower East Side Ann-Margret. All right, Rita Hayworth. (To Pablo) And you, fuzzy-top! Listen, I want both of you to meet—I want you to meet—

> HE steps through the table, is alone on stage, does a dance of love.

I want you to meet my silence and my surrender. I want you to meet the soft centre of the universe. I want you to meet the proof and the power, the brief and the everlasting—I want you to meet us. I want us to meet you. I want us to meet. I want everyone to meet everyone—I want everyone to be in love—with everyone—forever.

> His dance has led back to the table. HE takes the lover's hand and continues.

Gene. Pablo. I want you to meet—us. Oh, thank you, but we can't. We've finished eating and we have to get through a movie. We—

> HE and the lover stroll, skip, play games, chase each other, dance through an imaginary lovers' city.

—didn't like the movie. We found a nice little restaurant that we like. We just hate the new wide ties. We opened the window last night after making love and the people across the courtyard were playing the same record that we were. We may not be able to come to your party. We may never go out again. We have to get around to washing the dishes some week. We tried to pick up a cop and teach him love. We made a cab driver stop his cab and turn his radio up loud and we got out and danced and danced in the streets! We had a little fight. We made it up in bed. We made a date to have another fight. We took kown our Simon and Garfunkel poster and put up a Laurel and Hardy. We—we—we . . . (In ecstasy) We, we, we . . . You . . . I . . . Oh . . . You . . . I—OUI! We, wee, weeeeeeee (Runs and leaps over the chair. Husky)—all the way home.

> To the lover in the audience.

These are the things that you probably remember, and probably want to forget—the things that I should try to remember, and forget so easily—but I—

4

HE reaches out, the palms gesture, and quickly retracts his hands, holds them above his head like a prisoner, then like a girder, turning his feet out in fifth position, making a big "I".

I'm just a poisoner of love. I. I. The first person. Singular. The first position. The erect pronoun! I—I—ay-ay-ay-ay-ay. (Strolls) I am making ends meet. I miss you very much. I am working on a new play. I still haven't done the dishes. I am catching up on the art galleries. I saw a truly exciting new film. I am so interested in the new cinema. I started a fad by not wearing shoes. I'm still letting my hair grow. I wonder who's kissing her now. I—

HE has become chic and false. HE drops it and stares at the lover in the audience.

I couldn't watch the moon flight on television. It seemed so meaningless and repetitious. Because I—months before it happened—I—I had already crossed a more dangerous space—

HE begins a slow moonwalk toward the audience, his movements becoming slower and more stylized as his voice grows louder and more desperate.

I reached out and I crossed the space between one person and another. I with no machines to guide me. I with no home base to return to. I without special equipment. I with no scientific knowledge. I after watching hundreds of untrue training films. I with my naked body exposed. I with no maps or compasses. I with nothing to guide me but poems and fables and myths and songs and superstitions of a thousand years, I, alone, I, fearless, I, heroic, I reached out, I crossed that space, I travelled that void, and I touched you—

HE has become a bellowing madman and, just as it seems HE must fall into the audience, HE falls backwards, continuing the "Oooo" sound of the word "you" and transforming it into screams, cries, choked terrifying strangling sounds; his arms grab his chest as if in pain, then remain there as if in a straitjacket, he flops and buckles all over the stage, knocking the chair over, ending, in hideous whimpers, in a foetal position. HE suddenly snaps to attention, looking around at the audience and at imaginary people on stage like someone having to apologize for a terrible scene, someone having to prove his sanity. Slowly the straitjacket comes off and HE grows in confidence.

I—I'm all right now. I—I feel a lot better. Honest, I do. I—I think I can stand now without help. I—I realize I've been very injurious and immature in my relationships and that I've been evading reality. I see now that I was trying to hold on to a segment of my past that is—irretrievably gone—and I've been making myself and those around me who do care for me in their own way—unhappy due to my stubborn refusal to accept the fact that a certain period of happiness—which was very beneficial to my mental health while it lasted—has passed! And I've been making it impossible for myself to experience the good results and pleasant memories that might accrue from this—experience— because I kept trying to re-create it or to pretend that it could happen again, and—well, I'm babbling senselessly, aren't I?

    HE picks up the chair, sets it in place.

I guess what I'm trying to say is that I now DO feel myself in a much better state of mind to face the strains of everyday life. I regret most of all that my social relationships have deteriorated during this period of strain. I want very much to renew my relationships, to make new ones, I want to reclaim my place among my peer group, gang, I want to—(Fully his "showbiz" self) I wanna throw a PARTY!

    HE is now in his apartment.

Oh, God, there's the buzzer, and me not half-undressed!

    Runs over to buzz a visitor in. Addresses lover in audience.

Look, I'm going to show you what happened to us, and how it looked and felt to me, and maybe afterwards you'll tell me how it was for you. But while this first guest is climbing the stairs, let me tell you—I've had to take events that happened over a long period of time and compress them into one evening, and I've had to invent a few things that never happened at all, and I've even changed the apartment around—I mean, I've put the bathroom where the kitchen was, and vice-versa—but—I don't think there's anything basically false in it. I don't think there's anything in it to hurt or embarrass you—because I love you—and—for me—the first rule of love is that you never—never cause the one you love—any suffering you can spare them. (To rest of audience, quickly) I feel the same way about theatre! Oh, there's the first guest. It was Tom, I think—

6

HE opens the door, dazzlingly "showbiz." HE speaks before Tom
can say a word.

You haven't said a thing about my hair! (Laughs, embraces Tom) Hi,
numbskull, how are you, you look wonderful. Younger than Marlene
Dietrich. You're the first here. What's that? A six-pack. How sweet.
You didn't have to. I've got tons of cheap wine. (Puts beer in
refrigerator) Want one now? I'll have one, too. I hate that wine I got.
(Opens two beers) Now look, love, here's ya beer. I've got to get
dressed, so throw on a record and let people in, that's a dear. I appoint
you official doorkeeper while I make myself beautiful.

Goes into bathroom. HE faces a full-length mirror which is the
audience.

Oh, that's beautiful, Tom. I love that record.

It is "The Great Mandella" by Peter, Paul and Mary. HE hums
snatches of it while HE undresses, sips his drink. Occasionally HE
yells to Tom or the other guests as they come in.

That's the buzzer, Tom. La-da-da-da. Who is it? (HE is undressed,
checking his nakedness in the mirror, pulling in his stomach) Hi
yourself. I'm in here. I'll be right out. Get yourselves a drink. (HE
brushes his long hair vigorously) Who's that? Is that Billy? Get your ass
in here, toilet-tonsils! (HE admits Billy to the bathroom) Hi, shnooks.
Who'd you bring? (HE peeks out at Billy's date) Isn't he a little tall for
you? You need help? Oh, you brought help. (Takes a reefer from Billy)
He looks sweet, your friend. And any friend of yours is a friend of
mine. In fact, even if he was your blood enemy he could be a friend of
mine. My God, listen to those idiots pouring in out there. (Gives reefer
to Billy, resumes brushing his hair) What? No, he won't be here. If I
knew WHY he wouldn't be here, he'd be here, dunce. I haven't seen
him for—oh, a million years, I guess. Have you seen him? Is he all right?
Oh, what am I saying? Of course he's all right. Listen to me, trying to
take care of someone else when I can't even decide what to wear. Get
out there and make your friend comfortable—while I put on something
to make him uncomfortable. I'll be right out.

Billy leaves the bathroom. Still humming the song, He shakes his
hair, puts on a pair of shorts, rolls them up even shorter, selects
some beads and puts them on. HE flinches.

7

Cold beads!

> HE kisses himself in the mirror, picks up his beer and bursts out
> into the party.

Hey! How much bosom is it proper to show when you don't properly
have one?

> HE is the life of the party. Greets various guests.

Hello, world! Hi, how are you. My God, Joe, you're stoned! Oh, hi,
you're Billy's friend. Aren't you tall? Hey, you—I heard there was a big
party in your mouth last night!

> Music changes to "I'm So Glad You Came into My Life," by
> Blood, Sweat and Tears.

Hey, this is great for dancing—or cutting your throat. (Someone asks
about his hair) Yes, I'm letting it grow this time—till it reaches the
floor! Did you hear the one about the black hippie who let his hair grow
till it reached the ceiling? Hey, did Pablo and Gene come? I haven't
seen them for—oh, God, there's the door. Never mind, Tom, I'll get it,
you look very happy where you are—what I can see of you. (Buzzes
buzzer) Hey, big one, wanna dance with danger?

> HE is a swell dancer, and dances with a tall one. A sudden
> movement turns him to face the door, though across the room
> from it, and HE stops. The lover has come to the party. HE stands
> stone still and stops singing. The other guests leave the party.

(Distracted) Oh, goodbye. Goodnight. Yes, yes, I'll see you later.
Goodnight, Billy. Goodnight, Tom. Yes, later. At Wee Dick's? Fine. In
a while, maybe. Goodnight. Just close it behind you. Thank you.
Goodnight—

> HE is alone with the lover. They stand on opposite sides of the
> stage. HE starts to cross, then stops and grins as the lover
> undresses. HE unbuttons his shorts, lets them fall to the floor,
> kicks them away. HE takes off his beads, folds them in his hands,
> and drops them behind him. Then HE closes his eyes and advances
> across the stage. When HE reaches the spot where the lover stands,
> HE turns in space and slips into the lover's position. There is a

drastic light change. HE stands for a moment, poised, ecstatic, then stretches and yawns. It is later, after lovemaking. HE scratches himself, sensuously, like a cat, walks to a window, opens it, feels the breeze upon his body. HE turns and looks down at the floor, where the lover sleeps. HE turns on a small floor fan at the lover's feet, and adjusts it, feels it on his own hands and face. HE steps off the lover's height, measuring it against the length of his own feet. HE kneels beside his lover. The lover wakes.

Hi. Did I wake you? Did you know you're exactly five and one-half feet tall? My feet. (Kisses him gently) Hm? Oh, not late. Only about eleven. There's still time to go join the others, if you want. They're at Wee Dick's. A little bar. Where everyone goes right now. Sure, I want to go there. More than anything else in the world.

> Kisses him again, in caressing him accidentally touches his nipple.

I'm sorry. I forgot you were ticklish there. Let me kiss it and make it well.

> HE tries quickly and is lightly shoved away. HE laughs and then grows thoughtful.

I wonder why you're so ticklish there? I have a theory. I've thought about it a lot. I believe that when a person is supersensitive in a spot like that, it indicates some secret, some armoured muscle, some anxiety or neurosis that the person has. Let's try an experiment. No, no, I'm not going to touch it. Here, close your eyes. I promise I'm not going to touch it. Look, here's what I'll do. You can keep your hand on MY most sensitive spot. (Places lover's hands on his genitals) There. Now close your eyes and answer these questions. Do you believe that I love you?

> HE holds his hand high in the air, one finger pointing down at the lover's nipple, slowly, slowly brings it down. The lover answers "yes."

Good. Do you love me? ("Yes") Do you believe that love is important? ("Yes." Hand keeps coming down) Do you believe that the only reason that I want to know all about you and break through every secret and berrier between us is so that I can understand you and make you happier and protect you forever and ever? ("Yes") Then we should have no secrets? ("Yes")

> HE brings his finger down on lover's nipple. Lover reacts violently and squeezes AUTHOR'S genitals. AUTHOR gives a yelp of laughter and hops up.

Okay, okay, I'm sorry. I guess everybody has to have SOME secrets! Let's get dressed and take a shower and go over to Wee Dick's. You want to? I mean we're not going to accomplish anything else here for a while. (HE rubs his crotch) Not after that stunt. I am going to take a shower, since all my clothes are off, anyway. Waste not, want not, I say.

> HE enters bathroom, turn on water, feels it, adjusts it, climbs in. HE shouts off to the lover.

Everybody was asking about you before you came. No, Pablo and Gene weren't here. You like them, don't you? They'll probably be at the bar.

> HE soaps himself, intimately. Lover enters bathroom and turns light out.

Hey, what are you doing? Turn that back on! What are we playing, PSYCHO? (Lover climbs into shower) Here, don't rock the boat. (They embrace in the dark shower) Mmmmmmmmmm. (HE takes a mouthful of water, blows it at lover) That's for staying away so goddamned LONG. Listen, I'm getting out. The last time we did this I remember, we stayed in so long that when we got out we looked like we were wearing brocade jumpsuits. Let me go. (HE climbs out of shower, finds towel in the dark) I've just got one towel. I'm just using it to dry my hair. I'm putting it back on the rack. I'll dry the rest of me at the window.

> HE replaces the towel and goes into the other room, where between the fan and the window HE shakes himself dry like a dog. HE finds his shorts and beads and is slipping them on when the lover comes out of the bathroom.

Last chance. No? (Zips himself) Hey, can I wear your shirt? (Smells it) Mmmmmmmmmm. (Puts it on) You can wear one of mine. Or there's still a couple of yours in the closet. Why don't you leave your shoes here? I haven't worn any all summer. You could—pick them up tomorrow. (HE is trying to find out of the lover will be back) But do what you want to do. Come. Kiss me. Take my hand. Be brave. We're going to Wee Dick's!

> They kiss and HE takes lover's hand. They run downstairs and to the street. HE plays this whole speech to the audience, like a barker or a ringmaster.

What, oh what is Wee Dick's. It's the end of the world and the beginning of the next. It's the avant-garden of Eden! Say, if you want to know what Lower East Side life was like at the end of the Sixties, there's only one place to go. That's what it was like, there was only one place to go! You walk through streets filled with staggering drugged children, dressed like a Hollywood Halloween! They live on the streets. They don't go to movies, they don't go to plays—they don't want to see anything they haven't already seen on acid! You kick along through the lineup of cops and Buddhists, looking as freaky to them as they look to you, you wave at the Grey Line tourist bus, and suddenly there you are: Wee Dick's! It's got a simple sign in front, of glittering tinfoil coins and fuchsia neon, and inside, where the interracial rock makes conversation implausible, there's a short bar along one wall, then a crazy crowd dancing in the ultraviolet strobe light, and beyond that there's a few dark booths where you could sit if you could get through the dancers! So come in, world, there was no room to start with, come on in—to the only bar in New York with more customers than cockroaches—Wee Dick's!

> HE has shown the audience the layout of the bar, the bar itself along the rear wall, the entrance downstage where the bathroom mirror was, the dance floor taking up the other side of the stage. HE takes the lover's hand and they enter. HE waves a lot, squinting his eyes to see at whom.

Hello, everybody. I hear a lot of noise but I can't see a thing. Oh, honey, look, there in the booths at the back, I think I saw Pablo's hair in the strobe. Go see if he's with Gene; I'll get us some drinks. (Lover leaves. AUTHOR goes to bar.) Tom. Joe. Billy. Hi. Well, you didn't have to leave. You could have stayed and watched us fuck! My friend is here, he's back there hunting for Pablo and Gene. Huh? (Tom has pointed to Gene, sitting at the end of the bar) Hey, what's the matter with him? (HE goes to Gene's side) Gene, hi. Hey, what is this, you've

11

taken up drinking? Doesn't that contradict your macrobiotic bias? I
know, you're preserving your looks in alcohol. I wish I'd seen you when
we came in. My friend just went into the back to find you because I
thought I saw Pablo—HEY! BABY!

> Gene has knocked his bar stool over and fled. The AUTHOR runs
> after him, out the door, watches him run away down the street.
> HE returns to the bar. Picking up Gene's stool, to Tom:

Hey, what's the matter with him? He went down the street toward his
house like—what? Oh, no. Not him and Pablo. I can't believe it. They
were always like one person. Oh, God, I better go see Pablo. Even if I
have to cross that dance floor. Wish me luck.

> HE heads for the dance floor, the crossing of which is incredibly
> difficult. The music playing is Sly and the Family Stone's "Thank
> You For Letting Me Be Myself," so the dancing is hot and heavy.
> People grab the AUTHOR, try to get him to dance, even pinch
> him.

Hey, can an old man get through? Well, I'll be an old man by the time I
do. Hello, who ya dancin' with? Everyone? That's nice. Hey, let go of
me; you're not supposed to touch when you do the new dances. Well,
you're not supposed to touch ME! What happens if the music stops, do
we all fall down? I don't see how we could. Is it true there's a baby
born on this dance floor every two minutes? And it's a junkie in ten?
Hey, stop that. I'm old enough to be your father, and I don't want to.
So stop it. Hey, whaddaya know, he stopped.

> HE is finally across the floor, at the booths in the back. HE sees
> someone he knows.

Oh, hi. I'm looking for my friend, Pablo. He did? Damn. Did you see
my friend that came to the party? YOU know. Yes, I'm glad to see you,
too. 'Scuse me, I have to get back up front.

> HE dives back into the dancing mob as if it were a river.
> "Everyday People" is playing now.

Oh, God, I've got to order my next dancing crowd one size larger. This
is getting awfully tight. Who's got the football? Hey, I found a secret
passage, I can see light already. Or is it spots before my eyes?

HE is out of the mob again, crosses over to Tom.

Tom, do you suppose it's possible all of those people are just trying to get across the dance floor? (To someone else) Oh, hi, you're Billy's tall friend, aren't you? (To Tom) Did Pablo come up here? He did? Good. And did you see my friend? Oh, good. They probably went after Gene. I'll see you later. (To tall one) You're too big to be standing up, you know that?

Blows everybody a kiss and leaves the bar. HE looks in the direction that Gene went, sees nothing, shrugs, and turns to go back into the bar. HE sees something in the opposite direction. HE makes the palm gesture, automatically. HE turns, slowly, sadly, to face the lover in the audience. The palm gesture broadens into a huge shrug. HE drops his hands. To lover in audience:

When you see two people, walking that close together, and walking away that fast, they look—at first—like one person.

HE smiles sadly, lifts his hands once more in the palm gesture, keeps raising them, reaches into the air and takes down the "cigarette" and "drink" he placed there earlier, takes a sip of the drink, a drag from the cigarette, and smiles at the lover as the lights slowly fade.

13

'FRED AND HAROLD'
by Robert Patrick

The first performance in the United Kingdom of 'Fred and Harold' was
at The Ambiance Lunch-Hour Theatre Club (situated at Inter-Action's
Almost Free Theatre, Rupert Street, London W1) on Monday, 12th
May, 1975 with the following cast:

    Fred: Barry McCarthy
    Harold: Peter Whitman

An Inter-Action production directed by Stewart Trotter.

Approximate playing time: **10 minutes**

The apartment is swishy. FRED is strangling HAROLD. FRED wears a zipper jacket for cruising. HAROLD wears a robe and slippers.

FRED: Die, die, die, my delusions, die, die in my hands.

HAROLD: Guk-guk-guk-guk-guk!

FRED: (Drops HAROLD) Boy, whoever said violence was a sex substitute had just never had sex!

HAROLD: (Scuttling for safety) Get out. Get out of here. Help. Police. Help.

FRED: Oh, shut up. I'm not doing it anymore, am I?

HAROLD: (Who is far from door) Oh, God, I'm trapped.

FRED: Look, Henry, I'm not going to kill you, so just stop.

HAROLD: Harold. My name is Harold. Get out of here.

FRED: Oh, honestly. Harold, then. Have a cigarette. (Searches his pockets)

HAROLD: Have a cigarette?

FRED: DO you have a cigarette?

HAROLD: What are you doing here?

FRED: You think it's simple?

HAROLD: My God, two minutes ago you were trying to seduce me and all of a sudden you're beating me and now you want a cigarette?

FRED: I was not "trying to seduce" you; I offered to have sex with you. And I didn't beat you, I strangled you. And it was only an impulse and it might happen to anyone, and for Christ's sake, I STOPPED.

HAROLD: Oh, thanks a lot.

FRED: Now don't go hysterical on me. I need help with this thing.

HAROLD: I'm calling the police. (God knows how, as the phone is far away)

FRED: If you do, I'll tell them that you attacked me.

HAROLD: Me? You?

FRED: You were hitting at me. I'll bet I'm bruised.

HAROLD: Have YOU ever been trapped with an insane murderer?

FRED: Oh, I AM not. Jesus!

HAROLD: You better just go.

FRED: Look, will you talk to me?

HAROLD: (Sputters) What on earth can you want to TALK to me about?

FRED: Sex.

HAROLD: Leave me alone!

FRED: Look. If you let me stay, I promise I won't strangle you.

HAROLD: You'll have to make me a better offer than THAT.

FRED: You're marvellous with those cheap, conventional comebacks. I liked that about you right off at the party.

HAROLD: You know, you don't ACT crazy.

FRED: Will you believe that my trying to strangle you was just one of those wild coincidences that could never happen again? I mean—I never touched anyone violently in my life. It was—oh, symbolic. I don't think I could have done it even if you had been lighter.

HAROLD: Well, I'm fat, but that's not important.

FRED: You're not a bit.

HAROLD: Oh, I hate that. I am. I'm fat. I don't mind. I'm resigned to it. But go on.

FRED: You shouldn't feel that way about yourself. My God, I found you attractive, didn't I?

HAROLD: Hah! I know that look. I looked easy. You spotted me at that party and you thought: "Uh-huh. Fat. Easy lay." Ha! "Easy come, easy go." Don't hand me that. You tried and you fluffed it. Now—about that strangling?

FRED: Don't call it a strangling. I fluffed IT, too.

HAROLD: You're not going to do it again, are you?

FRED: I didn't want to do it in the first place.

HAROLD: Well, why did you do it, then? Did I invite it in some way?

FRED: It just seemed like the last straw. I came over here. I thought: "I'll give it one last try. Here's someone with sense who's had the same hard knocks I've had. He's hip. He's smart. He talks well, he's flip, he's fast, he's funny, he's cute—"

HAROLD: There you go again. I'm not. I'm not. There's no point in your saying that. I know I'm not. I don't brood about it anymore, but you really insult my intelligence when you go on about my being cute like that.

FRED: You're cute to me.

HAROLD: You're cute to me, too, but I don't insult your intelligence about it.

FRED: We oughta get together.

HAROLD: Don't start that.

FRED: Of course, it would take guts.

HAROLD: I just don't think about that side of things anymore.

FRED: It can happen.

HAROLD: It can't happen.

FRED: Afraid to go against public opinion? Afraid to choose each other?

HAROLD: Against public opinion?

FRED: Sure, you know, like in the movies: "Two dogs like us daring to love one another against all the dictates of society."

HAROLD: You said you thought I was cute.

FRED: I do, that's why I'm here.

HAROLD: You don't; you said you thought I was a dog.

FRED: By THEIR standards.

HAROLD: Their whose?

FRED: Society's. The pretty people.

HAROLD: You don't think I'm pretty?

FRED: It's not the most important thing.

HAROLD: Why fool ourselves?

FRED: Why not fool ourselves?

HAROLD: (Not without affection) You talk like a thirty-year-old novel.

FRED: And you talk like a sixteen-year-old girl! Thirty years ago! Why can't we get together? Because it wouldn't be perfect?

HAROLD: No, we'd just come to hate each other.

FRED: Jesus, we already hate each other. A moment ago I was strangling you.

HAROLD: And here we are fighting. I just don't think it would work.

FRED: But it was only out of frustration that I was strangling you.

HAROLD: See? You DID think I was an easy lay!

FRED: Well, yes.

HAROLD: Well, I'm not.

FRED: You're fighting me.

HAROLD: Not anymore. I'm throwing you out. And you're lucky I haven't called the police.

FRED: Look, I DON'T think you're an easy lay.

HAROLD: Do you think I'm coy?

FRED: No, just terribly afraid of being hurt. I understand that.

HAROLD: You do?

FRED: I've been hurt myself.

HAROLD: I don't know about you. You seem so brutal, and yet . . . Brutal and brittle. An interesting combination.

FRED: It takes courage to take the chance of getting hurt again.

HAROLD: Ha! Yes, it was brave of you to come over.

FRED: It was brave of you to ask me.

HAROLD: No, it wasn't. I never dreamed you would.

FRED: Do I have to go?

HAROLD: No point in your staying.

FRED: No point in anything.

HAROLD: We have to learn to live with it.

FRED: But why not together?

HAROLD: I'm not pretty.

FRED: Neither am I, particularly.

HAROLD: Well, there's that, too.

FRED: Just give me five minutes.

HAROLD: Of what, karate? (Laughs, relaxes) What is it you want to say?

FRED: Look, I'm a grown man—

HAROLD: A grown YOUNG Man.

FRED: —you're a grown man—

HAROLD: How old do you think I am?

FRED: It's hard to tell.

HAROLD: Guess.

FRED: I can't, really.

HAROLD: You'd better go. (Opens door)

FRED: Twenty-eight?

HAROLD: (Closes door) Thirty!

FRED: Really?

HAROLD: I don't worry about it.

FRED: You don't need to.

HAROLD: But I wish I would age. I mean, I'd lose hope then.

FRED: Yeah, nothing kill you like hope.

HAROLD: I just want—peace, now.

FRED: I agree.

HAROLD: No false hopes.

FRED: I know what you mean.

HAROLD: So you better go.

FRED: I guess you're right, it's hopeless. (Starts to go)

HAROLD: Oh, don't say that.

FRED: Why? I thought something could happen. I thought this might be it. I even felt a funny kind of—music—underneath it all. Not Wagner, maybe. But something quiet, throbbing. The "Bolero," maybe.

HAROLD: Please don't.

FRED: You feel something. I know you do.

HAROLD: It's understandable. I'm frustrated.

FRED: So am I.

HAROLD: See? You came just because of that.

FRED: Well, what are you frustrated because of?

HAROLD: Oh, because of myself, I know, I know. But I won't be had like that!

FRED: Like how, then? Tell me!

HAROLD: I've—I've learned to live without love.

FRED: You know, this kind of talk is why I strangled you before.

HAROLD: I can't open myself up to somebody and risk being hurt!

FRED: Look, let's screw.

HAROLD: I'm sorry.

FRED: Let's travel life's road together. Let's lift one another to the heights. Let's pretend. Let's fall in love. However you want me to put it. This is ridiculous. Our youth is flitting away while the blood clots and the flesh curdles. I'll do. You'll do. Let's.

HAROLD: It wouldn't come to anything.

FRED: It'd come to a climax.

HAROLD: No, please go, now.

FRED: Oh, hell, all right. (As a compliment) It was sure worth a try.

HAROLD: I hope I haven't hurt your feelings.

FRED: Yes, but.

HAROLD: I shouldn't think you'd have any trouble finding someone. Strong as you are.

FRED: Yeah? (HE is at door, turns)

HAROLD: I understand why you got so violent—

FRED: (Leans against door) You do?

HAROLD: I've felt that way, myself. (HE has been idly coming nearer)

FRED: Look, may I just kiss you goodnight?

HAROLD: Better not.

FRED: Why?

23

HAROLD: It'd just start things again.

FRED: It would?

HAROLD: Uh-huh.

THEY stand smiling at each other as the lights slowly fade.

'THINKING STRAIGHT'
by Laurence Collinson

to Drew Griffiths
who directed it as we both wanted

The first performance of 'Thinking Straight' was at The Ambiance
Lunch-Hour Theatre Club (situated at Inter-Action's Almost Free
Theatre, Rupert Street, London W1) on Monday, 10th March, 1975,
with the following cast:

> Laurence: Anthony Sher
> Man: Peter Small
> Young Woman: Linda Beckett

An Inter-Action Production designed by Norman Coates and directed
by Drew Griffiths

Approximate playing time: 40 minutes

The set consists of two television screens with a room in between. These are, in effect, three spaces which suggest, by scaffolding or whatever simple means appeals to the designer, that the audience may be able to watch two television programs simultaneously, as well as see the programs' author, Laurence, at work in his room. The screens converge slightly toward each other, and their adjacent sides frame the workroom, the function of which is clear from the desk, typewriter, and chair contained therein; extras such as books, desk lamp, files and so on, can be added according to the designer's wishes and/or available space.

Each of the television 'rooms' is a mirror-image of the other. They are bedrooms or bedsits, again according to the designer's preferences. The basic items of furniture in each are a divan, a bedside table on which are a lamp and a telephone, and a wastepaper basket. The single exit from each is a doorway. There are no solid walls or doors that will prevent the audience seeing the characters or the characters seeing one another.

> There are three actors on stage. The YOUNG WOMAN, and the MAN, in his mid-thirties, are asleep on their respective divans. The latter bears some resemblance to the ten-year-older LAURENCE, balding, bespectacled, and a little plump, typing in his workroom. Syrupy 'romantic' music can be used to create 'atmosphere' for the YOUNG WOMAN'S 'love story' at appropriate times. The director can also project suitable slides and/or film on to a backdrop, if he so wishes.

> Music. Soft lights go up on LAURENCE typing and the MAN and the YOUNG WOMAN asleep.

LAURENCE: (practising his beautiful title) The Moods of Love. The Moods of Love. The Moods of Love.

> LAURENCE starts to type again, but as his hands descend on to the keys, the typewriter gives out lush chords of slushy music. A spot on the YOUNG WOMAN as she wakes and starts to speak, at which point the typing becomes mime.

YW: I always dreamed I'd own a room
      in which, unfearing, I'd consume
      lovers innumerable and new

and old and faithful and untrue;
lovers in leisure and in haste;
lovers to fit my ample taste;
lovers who want to THIS or THAT
in the bed or on the mat,
upright or horizontally—
the angle's all the same to me;
lovers to kiss, to clasp, to crush;
lovers austere or lovers lush;
lovers who whisper or who roar;
lovers who tease—but none who bore;
lovers shy or rough; above
all other lovers those who LOVE;

And here I am in my perfect room
with bed and mat and cleansing broom,
docile colours and blending drape,
bread and wine and hanging grape
and books and prints and light and air:
fair setting for a game so fair;
a lamp to hush the atmosphere;
a door to lock when love is near;
walls so thick that who can pry?
a secret place where who can spy?
and here my every lover thrives . . .

but O! on waking, none arrives.

She opens her mouth to continue but can't think what to say.

What do I do next;

LAURENCE: I'm still trying to work it out. (Pause.) Let's keep on with the old version for now; you ought to remember that.

YW: But it's ten years ago.

MAN: (who has woken up) Why should she remember—she's only a puppet.

LAURENCE: Nonsense! She's a fully realised, in-depth character, created by an artist with sincerity and skilled craftsmanship. She is

young love, doomed by inexorable fate. She is the idealistic
heroine, destined for tragedy . . .

MAN: She's a puppet.

LAURENCE: Look, I told you to keep out of this. If I'd written it the
way it really was, which I'm about to do, only you keep
interfering, the play would never have got on the box. (To
YOUNG WOMAN) Let's get on, shall we? You're in this big city.
London, it was. Lots of exterior shots of busy streets and tall
buildings to show where you were. Then we zoomed across to the
building you lived in, and then tracked into your room.

Your opening bit was a piece of light verse, to catch the attention
of the viewers—hopefully! If they'd thought they were going to
get serious poetry, they'd have switched off and run a mile. But
this next poem is serious, and shows how lonely you are amid the
multitudes. Okay?

YW: Okay. (Pause)
        This is a city where a million sleep;
        This is my city where my life is linked
        to a million other lives by scars as deep
        as scars of history, and as distinct.
        Here I recognise a thousand faces:
        casual as leaves they brush my mind.
        Here I wander in a hundred places
        and meet a hundred comrades of my kind.
        Here there are, say, half a dozen friends
        who seek for me, or I them, in distress
        (a friend is one who uncorrupted tends
        compassion in a time of loneliness).

As the YOUNG WOMAN speaks the verses, she dresses as for
a party. She hears party dance music, circa 1964. Party
voices. LAURENCE picks up an appropriately clad male
dummy from a corner where it was partially concealed and
seats it across from the YOUNG WOMAN. She addresses the
final couplet to the dummy.

YW:
        A city's million, and I spurn them all;
        they speak in silence when I hear you call.

MAN: Hollywood shit.

LAURENCE: Okay, it's Hollywood shit. But that's the way it was for me. I used to go to the cinema, once a week at least. So all my life I've been looking for that stranger across a crowded room—or a crowded cottage.

MAN: Quite a few DISenchanted evenings.

LAURENCE: I learned from Hollywood that love is often found in the most UNEXPECTED places. Look at Bette Davis, Joan Crawford, Marlene—Hollywood Queens every one of them, and they always found lovers at the most INCONVENIENT times. Like in 'Now Voyager', when Bette meets Paul Henreid on that boat and says . . .

YW: Just a minute, just a minute. I thought I was the heroine. You're not giving me much of a chance, are you?

MAN: I'M the heroine.

LAURENCE: (To YOUNG WOMAN) Ignore him. Now, where were we? In the original script there was this whole series of shots to show how happy you were to have found a lover. You went tripping through the park, you gazed rapturously up at the trees with their autumn foliage, you stared with an inner glow of happiness across the lake, you touched a flower tenderly . . .

MAN: What brand of cigarette were you selling?

LAURENCE: It was really artistic.

MAN: Every packet of art should carry a government health warning.

LAURENCE: But there just isn't time for us to go over all that. Next came a sequence called The Simple Activities of Lovers.

MAN: Screwing.

LAURENCE: (scornfully ignoring the comment) Bus rides, eating together in restaurants, running hand in hand along a deserted beach, speeding along in a sports car, a radiant embrace with the camera revolving round you endlessly . . .

MAN: That's familiar.

LAURENCE: This was two years before 'A Man and a Woman' was released.

MAN: It still sounds like a commercial.

LAURENCE: I wasn't selling anything.

MAN: You were selling heterosexual sex, nineteen-sixties vintage.

YW: I like it. I am heterosexual. Can I do some more?

LAURENCE: Well, I'm still very fond of one of the sonnets . . .

> As the YOUNG WOMAN soliloquizes, LAURENCE goes and picks up the dummy and holds it so that she can address the poem to it. At the final couplet the YOUNG WOMAN floats into the dummy's embrace and whirls round and round with it, perhaps to the theme of 'A Man and a Woman'. LAURENCE returns to his desk when she has taken the dummy.

YW:
> Often in and out of love I'd skid
> and try to brake my heart, and break my heart,
> till screeching nightmares cluttered up my id
> and wrecked my life—at any rate, in part!
> So easily love punctured me, it seemed
> that Cupid was an over-active lout;
> but once in love, my reason was redeemed:
> I found I just as easily fell out.
> That's how I know I am as serious
> in loving you as ever I can be;
> reason and time find I'm impervious;
> love has become invulnerable in me,
> and in this land whose enemy connives
> ineptly, it learns fortitude, and thrives.

> The MAN has risen from his divan and is taking off his clothes.

LAURENCE: Hey, what are you doing?

MAN: Getting ready for the obligatory full-frontal.

LAURENCE: But there wasn't any sex. At least, not like that. And there isn't going to be any now.

MAN: Of course not. It was all yearning faces and bodies in dark silhouette, wasn't it?

LAURENCE: What if it was? The oblique approach is usually more artistic than the explicit.

MAN: Balls!

LAURENCE: So I see.

MAN: You weren't only selling straight sex, you were even being hypocritical about that.

LAURENCE: Television is a family medium.

MAN: Blah, blah, blah! Since when have you been protecting the nuclear family?

LAURENCE: Gay liberation hadn't even been thought of then. Nor women's lib.

MAN: But you'd been a gay activist.

LAURENCE: In a small way. Collecting pennies for the Albany Trust. I still had so many hang-ups . . .

MAN: You were a coward.

LAURENCE: Yep. And I also knew that at that time there was no chance of getting a gay play on TV. At least, not one that took for granted that gay feelings were natural. I could speak my emotions about love, but not about the love that dared not speak its name. But that was really what I dealt with, so it didn't matter.

MAN: Rationalisations.

LAURENCE: (to YOUNG WOMAN) Go on, please, It IS the sex scene, and it IS in shadow.

The two television rooms darken, with spots on the faces of
the YOUNG WOMAN and the MAN. She is lying on her
divan, and the MAN is lying on his, but she has the dummy
with her, most of their two torsos under the bedclothes. She
is, however, propped up on her elbow, contemplating her
'lover'.

YW: The dawn is hesitant and so must creep
greyly to the shadows of the room.
The light betrays two lovers: one asleep,
breathing, dreaming, haloed in the gloom
by the other's arm; this other one awake,
intent on her beloved's tranquil face,
wondering, as lovers do, that . . .

MAN: (roaring) NO!

LAURENCE: Go on.

YW: . . . wondering, as lovers do, that it should make
perfection for her; then her fingers trace . . .

MAN: No, no, no! Give me some light!

The lights go up. The music stops. While speaking, the MAN,
still naked, crosses the stage.

LAURENCE: Get back where you belong, will you, please.

MAN: When I've got what I want.

LAURENCE: You do what I want.

MAN: Of course. I'm part of you, and I want what you want—whether
you know it or not.

The MAN goes to the young woman's divan, hauls up the
dummy, and takes it back to his own divan.

MAN: I'll tell you how it really was.

The MAN sprawls beside the dummy, both of them

uncovered and naked. Lights down, music up, spots on him
and the dummy only. When he speaks, he must stress the
pronouns

MAN: The dawn is hesitant and so must creep
greyly to the shadows of the room.
The light betrays two lovers: one asleep,
breathing, dreaming, haloed in the gloom
by the other's arm; this other one awake,
intent on HIS beloved's tranquil face,
wondering, as lovers do, that it should make
perfection for HIM; then HIS fingers trace
the shapes of eyes, mouth, brow, and nose
—a scurry of air rather than a touch,
lest HE disturb HIS lover's white repose—
and to HIMSELF HE says: 'This is as much
as ever I have wanted,' and HE lays
HIS head beside HIS lover's, settles deep
into a joy beyond HIS power to phrase;
and as the day is poised, two lovers sleep.

The MAN nestles down beside the dummy for a few seconds
as the music dies away, then, as the lights go full on, he
stands up with the dummy in front of him, its face toward
the audience. Their pose is one of anal sex. As he speaks, the
dummy has a full erection.

MAN: And we didn't sleep much that night, either.

LAURENCE: PUT . . .THAT . . .AWAY!

MAN: Don't YOU get a hard-on in similar circumstances?

LAURENCE: That's not the point.

MAN: It's exactly the point. Funny thing about contemporary life. The
hard prick, which, mistakenly or not, is probably humanity's most
dominating and obsessive symbol, is mostly ignored or regarded as
comical. Maybe because it's so serious.

LAURENCE: Nevertheless, one doesn't show such things in . . . in . . . what shall we call it?—in the performing arts.

MAN: Why not? One shows everything else in life: washing dishes, washing hair, slapping faces, stabbing, shooting, murdering, dying, stoning babies, gouging eyes, kisses, embraces. The only other significant taboo I can think of is shitting on stage, though there's plenty of verbal shit around any theatre. The central, the essential fact of sex and love and sexual love—(Gently:) other than between lesbians—is that men have penises; and if those penises can't get hard enough, there just can't be any relationship.

YW: (Indignantly starting to come over) Cock!

MAN: Pardon?

YW: Cock! What you're talking! I want to point out that . . . that . . . (As her face moves unintentionally close to the dummy's penis, the YOUNG WOMAN becomes momentarily confused.) cocks are NOT essential to good love-making—not to women, anyway. A eunuch, if he wants to, can make a woman feel marvellous . . .

LAURENCE: (incredulous) Really . . . ?

YW: Yes! Simply by touching, caring, being LOVING.

MAN: That sounds a bit like lesbian politics. Are you a . . . ?

YW: I'm a woman—with all sorts of potentialities.

LAURENCE: You're holding things up. Please get back on your own side.

YW: (retreating with dignity) Just as you're a man, with all sorts of potentialities too; toward women as well as men.

LAURENCE: All right, all right, but that's for another script. (He picks up the dummy, but in returning it to the YOUNG WOMAN he accidentally thrusts its penis at her crotch. He hastily but unsuccessfully attempts to put the penis back inside the trousers.) Here, it's your turn to play with Sir John.

YW: (Triumphantly drawing the zip over the penis) Cocks aren't everything.

LAURENCE: Please . . .

YW: You see, some subjects ARE unmentionable, even to liberationists. (She places the dummy on her own divan in an attitude of sleep. Dressed now in a robe, she gazes down at it soulfully, but suddenly looks up again at LAURENCE and the MAN.) We really don't see eye to eye—on practically anything.

> LAURENCE shrugs despairingly. The YOUNG WOMAN gestures as if to say: 'I've said my piece', and strikes a soulful attitude again. At this point the dummy gives the first of a series of increasingly loud snores.

YW:
> No, no, I see it differently from you.
> We'd best define our terms. YOU speak of lust;
> I: love; the argument is far from new;
> its relevance, though, is golden through the rust.
> I can't deny that passion's there in both;
> that's how we are, and who would have it other.
> But it's a surface joy—only to clothe
> the soul of love—and overmuch will smother.
> You claim it's ALL: the universe of love!
> O what a paltry bedroom place you're at!
> I suppose when passion's done you like to walk
> away. Or—at the best—you grunt and puff
> and fall asleep and that's the end of that.
> But if you LOVED, you'd lie awake and talk.

> As the sonnet ends, she shakes the dummy in fury, then, exhausted, collapses miserably downstage. LAURENCE, overcome with emotion, congratulates her.

LAURENCE: Thank you. Very nice. That, of course, was the first indication that all wasn't going smoothly in this affair.

MAN: (Putting his clothes back on) And it's the same old affair.

LAURENCE: Meaning?

MAN: The same old GAY affair, predestined to break up before it gets started. The Well of Loneliness, The Boys in the Band, Quatrefoil, Finistere, and dozens of other gay classics that prove that the gay life is essentially tragic.

LAURENCE: All life is essentially tragic. We start to die as soon as we're born.

MAN: But the period in between doesn't have to be spent feeling miserable.

LAURENCE: Anyway, a gay relationship isn't so very different from a straight one—in terms of happiness and emotional security. How many straight marriages fall apart; just look at the divorce statistics. And those that don't are usually held together by children or legal contracts or property ownership. At least gay relationships are honest—in comparison.

MAN: Your arguments are as stereotyped as your story. Gay relationships can't be honest as long as gays want to pattern them on straight relationships.

YW: There's nothing wrong with straight relationships . . .

LAURENCE: Except that most of them are crooked.

YW: And so are most gay relationships.

MAN: Because gays model themselves on the man-and-wife family unit. The fact is . . .

LAURENCE: Bring on the soapbox!

MAN: I don't need one. The man-and-wife family unit—the nuclear family—whatever you want to call it—exists today, not to give security to children, which it can hardly be said to do efficiently anyway, but to keep our authoritarian social structure from falling apart. (The YOUNG WOMAN turns away with boredom.) There's no need for gays to emulate heterosexual marriage, unless they themselves are as hung up as straights about Dominating Daddies and Meek Mummies. We should, ideally, be able to let relationships depend purely on our need to care, for ourselves and for others; and on our physical and intellectual needs. Not on family conditioning, not on social conditioning . . .

LAURENCE: But where does the conditioning start and where does it stop?

MAN: Ay, there's the rub.

LAURENCE: You've dragged a lot of politics into what was a simple romantic story.

MAN: Romance IS politics. Always. Read Reich.

YW: For Christ's sake, what am I supposed to be doing while you two squabble.

LAURENCE: You're quite right. Let's get on.

LAURENCE: The girl by then had begun to realise that her lover wasn't precisely the answer to a maiden's prayer.

MAN: And she was no maiden, either.

LAURENCE: She was the sort of person who loved totally . . .

MAN: You?

LAURENCE: Of course. While he, well, love was okay—in its place.

MAN: ,   'Man's love is of man's life a thing apart,
          'Tis woman's whole existence.'
          Byron—Don Juan.

LAURENCE: You could say that.

MAN: Talk about conditioned role-playing!

LAURENCE: I wrote quite a spectacular little scene to illustrate that. It was a bit like a Chagall painting—the lovers flying together in the air, hand in hand, and then settling slowly on the peak of a mountain.

YW: The lovers flew to the peak of the world
              where they perched and pecked;
         the waves and cities and angels swirled
              about them: a brilliant prospect.

         Then when the sexual havoc fled
              and the firmament stilled,
         Lover turned to Other and said:
              'My life has been fulfilled.'

         Other closed an eye and spied
              at the shivering sky,
         thought ten seconds, then replied:
              'The stars are very high.'

         Lover exclaimed: 'I love you so;
              you leave, I weep';
         Other watched the rivers flow:
              'The sea is very deep.'

         Saddened lover: 'I wish I knew
              you loved me.' Other sighed
         and gazed ahead: 'Of course I do.
              The world is very wide.'

LAURENCE: She was terribly unhappy. She could sense that he
wanted to keep his distance from her—and she didn't know how to
cope. She wrote him letter after letter, but she never posted one of
them.

        The MAN picks up his own wastepaper basket, which
        contains dozens of sheets of crumpled notepaper, then, with
        an ironic smile, picks out the sheets one by one and casually
        tosses them on the floor.

MAN: He loves me, he loves me not, he loves me, he loves me not, he
loves me, . . .

        Meanwhile the YOUNG WOMAN has been writing a letter.
        She glances through it, then crumples it up and throws it in
        her wastepaper basket. She retrieves it, reads it through
        quickly and hopelessly, then gazes soulfully into space.

LAURENCE: Although there were moments of fulfilment . . .

YW: I thought I knew how grossly love could grieve:
          the furnace in the belly; and the fears
          ribboning from the brain to interweave
          my sudden and unreasonable tears.
          'No more!' I said. 'I'll never love again
          unless I'm loved before. My destiny
          must be my own. Why should I plead for pain
          when I can shrug my shoulders and be free?'
          Thus went my argument; now I'd smile
          if I'd the heart, but that escaped to you;
          reason has become an imbecile;
          and I, fanatic, find my grief anew;
          returning but to transitory calm
          held in the doubtful harbour of your arm.

> As the YOUNG WOMAN starts this last poem, LAURENCE
> picks up the dummy again and, as soon as she reaches the
> word 'free', he 'knocks' on her door. She hesitates
> uncertainly, but finally opens up. Seeing her 'lover' there, she
> grasps 'him' in her arms. LAURENCE retreats to his
> workroom as she finishes the poem.

LAURENCE: But it was a one-sided affair. Oh, yes, he felt a vague
affection for her, but nothing like her love for him.

MAN: Oh, yes.

LAURENCE: She would have left him if she'd had the will-power, but
she was in too deep.

MAN: Silly bitch.

LAURENCE: As I said—a classical situation. She knew that the only
way she could keep him was to keep her emotions hidden as
much as possible, though she was longing desperately for some
sort of equality of love. You may be wondering why he didn't just
piss off . . .

MAN: Because SHE was a good fuck.

LAURENCE: I'D like to think so. But he wasn't a totally unfeeling
brute.

MAN: (affectedly) Just a typical man, darling!

LAURENCE: One of the functions of the script—it was for an experimental slot, by the way, and very lucky I was to have been offered it; imagine if I'd tried to make it gay; in England; in 1964 B.B.

MAN: B.B.?

LAURENCE: Before the Bill. The script was an attempt to combine the imagery of poetry with the imagery of sight and sound. The director and I let our heads go with the next scene—about the Girl's disillusionment.

MAN: Ah, disillusion. Gay lovers were inevitably disillusioned.

LAURENCE: We had stock shots of sea and beach and rocks and waves and what-have-you. The viewers must have felt absolutely drenched.

GIRL:　　　　The lover drowns as dreams capsize;
　　　　　　troubling waves like time in flood.
　　　　　　Her daily boat dissolves like blood
　　　　　　as past and future tempests rise.

　　　　　　You signalled (her considered view);
　　　　　　in your assurance she set sail;
　　　　　　her foolish craft; for two, too frail . . .
　　　　　　her own fault; she invited you.

MAN: Not 'HER daily boat' but HIS; not 'HER considered view' but HIS; not 'SHE set sail' but HE; not, not, and not again; not 'SHE invited you' — HE did.

LAURENCE: I admit it.

MAN: Not a bad poem, though.

LAURENCE: Thanks. I like it.

MAN: Are there any you write that you don't like?

LAURENCE: It happens—occasionally.

MAN: So what comes next?

YW: I'm betrayed.

LAURENCE: Oh, good, you've remembered.

YW: Betrayal always comes next in a standard love affair.

LAURENCE: (to the MAN) You see, there's a classical sequence.

MAN: A cliché sequence, you mean. Especially for a gay affair.

LAURENCE: For ANY affair. You've no idea how many people—
straights, I mean—told me that The Moods of Love—that's what I
called the script—was a reflection of their own experience.

MAN: And that made you feel good?

LAURENCE: Of course.

MAN: You didn't think you were misleading people?

LAURENCE: By telling the truth?

MAN: Was it the truth?

LAURENCE: That's a perfect "non sequitur". How am I supposed
to answer?

MAN: Honestly. Only, of course, you can't.

LAURENCE: I'm dishonest?

MAN: No, ignorant. To my mind, being gay isn't just a matter of sexuality.

LAURENCE: That's hardly headline news.

MAN: Maybe not. But a gay man or woman has to consider his or her sexuality in far wider terms than straights think about theirs. In fact, straights don't HAVE to think about theirs. They grow up, taking for granted that it's okay to be heterosexual. They may, in our happy puritan heaven, have hangups about what they DO with their sexuality, but that's a different matter.

LAURENCE: I still don't understand how I'm supposed to have misled people. Infidelity is so common . . .

MAN: Infidelity equals unfaithfulness equals not keeping faith with a particular person. The implication is that being in love with or having sex with two or more different people at the same time is immoral.

LAURENCE: It's not?

MAN: No, it's not.

LAURENCE: I may perhaps agree with you intellectually, but my emotions aren't so easily persuaded. Be that as it may, infidelity, as I was saying, is so common—in straight and gay relationships both—that, well, there it was. In the penultimate sequence the Girl . . .

MAN: The Girl?

LAURENCE: All right, me. I. I saw him meeting another woman, obviously a new lover . . .

MAN: Woman?

LAURENCE: Another man. What's the difference? The FEELING'S the same. Such a to-do! Grey rainy weather, the depths of depression, the final realisation that it's all over. Must be.

YW: My love, my last love sonnet now, for you . . . (stops abruptly, then:) Oh, do I use masculine or feminine pronouns?

LAURENCE: (glancing hesitantly at the MAN) Well, I don't want another argument on such a trivial point . . .

MAN: Trivial, never. But to save time—say it as it was written.

YW:
My love, my last love sonnet now, for you:
each mourning word an elegy for youth;
for she is dying now who hardly knew
maturity, although she nuzzled truth.
I hug our yesterday, and wish you well,
her well-intentioned murderer; and yet
your casual treason gashed the flesh of hell,
and mind tormented minds, cannot forget.
And so, despite my love, this hope I own:
that you, like me, one darkening dawn will moan:

'Did I do this, to whom now this is done?'
And in betrayal handed on again
find the smashed sun astounding in your pain.

MAN: You had it bad, didn't you?

LAURENCE: A mild case of infatuation.

MAN: Mild? It sounds more like terminal.

LAURENCE: Alas, no. Just one of numerous such attacks.

MAN: A regular pattern.

LAURENCE: That's what I've been trying to tell you.

MAN: I bet you always said to yourself: 'I won't go to bed with anyone unless I really love him.'

LAURENCE nods.

MAN: Really, really love him.

LAURENCE: (Impatiently) Yes, yes, yes . . .

MAN: But on the side you had—as one of the twentieth century's more renowned closet queens phrased it—a series of brief encounters. A grope in a cottage, a pull at a party, a suck at a sauna . . .

LAURENCE: I didn't know about saunas then . . .

MAN: Don't quibble. Did you or didn't you have furtive flings?

LAURENCE: Is this or isn't it an inquisition?

MAN: You're always muttering about honesty and integrity . . .

LAURENCE: So what if I did have . . . furtive flings?

MAN: I'm not criticising. I'm merely pointing out the contradiction in your sexual philosophy. On the one hand an idealised, no doubt eternal . . .

LAURENCE: I prefer 'permanent' or 'semi-permanent'.

MAN: Your verbal precision does you credit.

LAURENCE: Thank you.

MAN: . . . a semi-permanent love affair; and on the other hand the immediate relief of urgent needs. Hypocritical or not?

LAURENCE: I'm cornered. Does that make you happy?

MAN: If only gays recognised the degree to which their sexual thinking is indocrinated in them by heterosexual mores. Inside every closet queen there's a male chauvinist pig snouting its way out.

LAURENCE: (drily) How exciting!

MAN: There's no reason for us to marry—we call it pair-bonding; we don't have to commit adultery; we don't have to be promiscuous. All these are hetero concepts based on the nuclear family tradition. We can have one lover or we can have ten or we can have a thousand . . .

LAURENCE: I should be so lucky.

MAN: . . . It's a matter of what we decide WE want; we don't have to give straight names to what we do or think of it in straight terms. It's enough for us to be LOVERS—the word 'love' meaning anything from a mild physical attraction to a deep and lasting friendship. Have you noticed how scared some gays are even to say the word 'lover'?

LAURENCE: I'm not, and I never have been.

MAN: No, I'll give you that—but most closet queens don't say: 'He's my lover' but: 'He's my affair'—or 'He's Tom's affair'—or 'Tom and Bill are an affair'. A couple can HAVE an affair, but nobody IS an affair. Some gays don't dare to think of themselves as being lovers; that's something only straights can be. Our relationships are really too distasteful or sordid to be described by such a beautiful word. Our huge self-hatred shows itself in so many tiny ways.

LAURENCE: Our? YOU dare to say OUR!

MAN: Oh well, I may sneer at the silly ostriches, but I don't reject them.

LAURENCE: (with slight indignation) Nor do I.

MAN: But you're still the man who wrote 'The Moods of Love' ten years ago.

LAURENCE: I'm ten years older. And I've come out to exactly the same extent as you. After all, you ARE me.

MAN: I'm your HEAD, but I'm not sure now that I'm YOU.

LAURENCE: Well, our feelings don't always travel the same road as our heads.

MAN: And I'm the—well—AVANT GARDE you: the one who goes to gay lib meetings, and reads the literature on women's politics, and puts down closeted gentlemen, and derides organisations that see no farther than tolerance and integration . . .

LAURENCE: In that case, who am I?

45

MAN: You're the mask that hides the timid man and the braggart writer. You're the typewriter that talks big but secretly wants a suburban romance and correct business meetings; you're the typewriter that taps out crusades but yearns for secure unrevolutionary contentment.

LAURENCE: With another typewriter?

MAN: You're an artist—and you're everyone and no-one.

LAURENCE: I'm a mess, obviously.

MAN: Now you must choose who and what you really want to be.

LAURENCE: From the way you talk, I suspect I've written one of those trendy plays about the crisis of identity.

YW: Not to mention the crisis in communication.

MAN: And alienation.

LAURENCE: And the breakdown of the hegemony established by functionalism . . .

MAN; YW: What!

LAURENCE: I read that on a Penguin blurb.

MAN: The play's a myth . . .

LAURENCE: And a manifesto . . .

YW: And an existentialist epic combining the theatre of cruelty with that of the absurd with that of naturalism and realism and expressionism and impressionism . . .

MAN: And linguistics and semantics and sociology and documentary.

LAURENCE: But there's one thing it won't be.

MAN; YW: What?

LAURENCE: (sadly) Commercial.

YW: Can I get away, please?

LAURENCE: Please stay. Since you're both me, I choose to be you two, too. And the hundred and one others who are part of me, also. I love you both.

MAN: Which means you love yourself.

LAURENCE: Yep.

YW: Which is a sort of . . . masturbation.

LAURENCE: What do you mean—sort of? Masturbation is marvellous. And so is sex—the whole spectrum—of which gay sex—according to Kinsey, sadly missed—provised a third to a sixth of the total. Which is an awful lot of sex; Suppose that, in just the United Kingdom, eight to ten million sex acts take place every night— that's a conservative estimate—then about a million of those fucks are going to be gay.

MAN: What a sublime thought!

LAURENCE: Gay IS sublime. Gay sex is sublime. Gay sex is beautiful. Gay is good. (Does wild little steps to the slogans:) Two four six eight, gay is just as good as straight. Out of the closets and into the streets.

MAN: Yes, into the streets.

YW: Can . . . can I come with you?

MAN: Why?

YW: Well, because . . . now I think I begin to understand what you've been talking about—I mean, about him (LAURENCE) . . . and oppression . . . and what the word really means. I ought to—after all, I am one of the SECOND sex.

MAN: Do YOU love yourself?

YW: I'm going to start to—right away. Do you?

The MAN nods with a smile.

LAURENCE: Do we love ourselves?

ALL: (a shout) Yes!

MAN: Then into the streets!

LAURENCE: Performing a masque—like the Elizabethans at the end of their plays.

YW: But wearing no masks. (She brushes her hands gently over her own and the MAN'S face, while the latter does the same to LAURENCE.)

MAN: (To LAURENCE) Yours has slipped a bit.

LAURENCE: I've written a song for it.

MAN: Called?

LAURENCE: Not sure yet. The gay gavotte. The troll's tango. The sissy shimmy . . .

MAN: . . the cocksucker's concerto. The fag fandango. The bugger's blues. The sodomite's serenade.

LAURENCE: Oh, I like that. (Pause) Sodomy serenade. Perhaps . . .

YW: That'd be all right for you two buggers, but what about me? (Looks down at their flies) I don't have the same equipment.

LAURENCE: Love always finds a way.

> The play closes with a little send-up (With sodomitical overtones) of a 'Thirties-type' Hollywood dance routine, each joining in as his/her turn comes to sing. Special effects can include the word 'LIBERATION' suddenly appearing on the TV screens as LAURENCE reaches the word in the first stanza. The YOUNG WOMAN can unveil a rainbow as she steps out to take her part in the threesome.

The song and dance routine are to the tune of 'That's Entertainment'.

LAURENCE:

> You damn
> Everything that I am;
> What I do
> May be not right for you;
> But agree
> You can just let me be—
> That's liberation.

LAURENCE, MAN:

> All said,
> While we're different in bed,
> We can claim
> In most ways we're the same;
> We're as true
> Human beings as you—
> That's liberation.

YW:

> I tagged you a fag and a fairy and queer,
> A queen unserene and a pansy, my dear,
> But gays in these days stop our liberal jeer;
> Why should we straights regret you—
>
> (Clasps both men to her breast)
>
> For did we not beget you?

ALL:

> Everyone
> Has a right to the sun
> And a place
> In the whole human race,
> So love proud
> With the rest of the crowd—
> Think straight and think gay;
> They both lead the way
> To liberation . . .

BLACKOUT

'SHIPS'
by Alan Wakeman

for Ed Berman

The first performance of 'Ships', three linked short plays for intimate theatre, was at The Ambiance Lunch-Hour Theatre Club (situated at Inter-Action's Almost Free Theatre, Rupert Street, London W1) on Monday, 31st March, 1975, with the following cast:

'Coffee'
    Houseman: Andrew Tourell
    Gasman: Anthony Smee

'Tea'
    Houseman: Andrew Tourell
    Tubewoman: Elaine Ives-Cameron

'Wine'
    Michael: Jim Duggan
    Dim: Iain Armstrong
    Streaky: Timothy Welsh
    Gasman: Anthony Smee
    Tubewoman: Elaine Ives-Cameron
    Roger: Barry Parman

An Inter-Action Production designed by Norman Coates and directed by Gerald Chapman

Approximate playing time: 50 minutes

'SHIPS'

First . . .
COFFEE
(We are in HOUSEMAN'S flat. It is morning)

Then . . .
TEA
(First in a tube station, then HOUSEMAN'S flat)

Finally . . .
WINE
(We are in a city park)

A great city multiplies chance encounters with strangers until they
become a daily commonplace. Yet every such chance encounter could
still be the beginning of a marvellous adventure. This is the excitement
of the city. This is why we put up with the noise and the dirt, the pace
and the pressure. How paradoxical then that we should spend so much
of our time pretending that those people queuing with us for the bus,
or sitting next to us in a restaurant, are not real people at all. How
paradoxical that we should shut ourselves off from them and behave as
if they, and we, were only cardboard cut-outs. For, like us, each one of
them has lived a life of 60-minute hours, 24-hour days, 365-day years,
year in and year out, leading inexorably to this particular moment
when we sit in this particular moment when we sit in this particular
theatre, waiting for this particular play to start . . .

COFFEE

> GASMAN: Cheeky/cheerful/20ish/Cockney
> HOUSEMAN: Serious/quiet/30ish

> HOUSEMAN's home. Morning. The doorbell rings.
> HOUSEMAN answers it.

GASMAN: Morning! Gasboard. Come to see about a leak.

HOUSEMAN: Oh yes. Come in. The kitchen's through here. I think I
know where the leak is, actually. It's that joint where the pipe
goes into the stove.

GASMAN: Right you are. Just leave it to me.

HOUSEMAN: I'll be in the other room if you need anything.

GASMAN: Right you are. Just leave it to me.

> GASMAN gets down to work. HOUSEMAN goes to other
> room to work on papers etc. After a moment, he gets up
> again and returns to speak to GASMAN.

HOUSEMAN: Er . . . Hallo . . . Er, it occurred to me you might like a
cup of coffee.

GASMAN: Wouldn't say no. Can't use the cooker though. I've 'ad to
turn off your stop-cock.

HOUSEMAN: Oh. That's all right. I'll use the electric kettle.

> HOUSEMAN fills kettle and plugs it in.

How long have you been doing this job?

GASMAN: Couple of years.

HOUSEMAN: Do you like it?

GASMAN: It's okay. Nothing to write 'ome about. The money's good. I'm not complaining.

HOUSEMAN: Do you always wear jeans to work in?

GASMAN: . . . Well, they're practical—and they're cheap.

HOUSEMAN: (Laughs) I don't think that's the only reason people wear them.

GASMAN: What other reason would there be?

HOUSEMAN: Well, some young men I know wear them because they think it makes them look . . . sexy.

GASMAN: (Laughs) If you're feeling sexy, it's a matter of taking things off, not putting them on, i'n'it?

HOUSEMAN: (Laughs) Yes.

Kettle boils.

GASMAN: Your kettle's boiling.

HOUSEMAN: What?

GASMAN: Your water—it's boiling.

HOUSEMAN: Oh, the water. Yes. Thanks.

HOUSEMAN prepares cups, makes coffee etc.

GASMAN: So . . . er . . . you reckon it makes me look sexy, do yer?

HOUSEMAN: I didn't say that. I said OTHER people . . .

GASMAN: Fellers are always making passes at me. I dunno why.

HOUSEMAN: I wonder why that could be . . .

GASMAN: Wha'd'yer mean? I don't encourage no one.

HOUSEMAN: Some people might find your manner of dress provocative.

GASMAN: I'm only wearing a pair of old jeans, for Chrissake!

HOUSEMAN: How do you like your coffee?

GASMAN: In a cup.

HOUSEMAN: I mean what do you want in it?

GASMAN: Oh the usual things. Arsenic. LSD. What yer got?

HOUSEMAN: I've got sugar and milk.

GASMAN: Yeah, well I'll 'ave both them.

      HOUSEMAN pours milk, picks up sugar bowl and taps it.

GASMAN: Two. There, that's done. Shouldn't 'ave no more trouble with that. Just needed a spot of grease up yer flexible 'ose.

HOUSEMAN: Oh. Thanks. Here's your coffee.

GASMAN: Ta. Nice place you've got 'ere. Is that a colour telly?

      HOUSEMAN takes his own coffee and returns to the other room.

HOUSEMAN: Yes, it is. I don't know why I have it really, the amount I watch.

GASMAN: I've never seen a colour telly working.

HOUSEMAN: Well I'm afraid you're out of luck. There's never anything much on at this time of day.

GASMAN: Lovely programmes in the evenings, though, aren't there? In the EVENINGS.

HOUSEMAN: Yes. Quite often there are.

There is a pause. They look at each other.

GASMAN: Well, I must be pushing off. Another lovely young 'ousewife is awaiting my services somewhere. Just sign 'ere

HOUSEMAN: (Signing) Thank you for doing the job so quickly. There's a very good film on BBC2 tomorrow evening, actually. If you're interested.

GASMAN: You don't say. Well, I might just pop in and watch it with you then.

HOUSEMAN opens door. GASMAN goes through it.

Keep smiling. Cause you're not so bad-looking yerself. You know . . . See yer!

GASMAN exits and immediately re-enters and rings the doorbell again.

GASMAN: Morning! Gasboard. (Aye aye! Bit smart in 'ere, i'n'it? Rich bastard) Come to see about a leak.

HOUSEMAN: (Christ! What a gorgeous boy!) Oh yes. Come in. The kitchen's through here. (Damn! Why must these temptations be thrust at me?) I think I know where the leak is, actually. It's that joint where the pipe goes into the stove. (Okay, so you're very sexy, but would I actually want to go to bed with you? That's the question)

GASMAN: Right you are. Just leave it to me. (One of them. I got your number matey. Fancy yer chances, do yer?)

HOUSEMAN: I'll be in the other room if you need anything.

GASMAN: Right you are. Just leave it to me.

GASMAN gets down to work. HOUSEMAN goes to other room to work on papers etc.

(Just look at this pad. Some people 'ave all the bleeding luck. I bet if I played my cards right I could really screw this geezer. 'E's bound to 'ave a go at me.)

HOUSEMAN: (I definitely won't make a pass at him. My life's far too complicated already. Still, I suppose it's only civilised to offer him some coffee.)

> HOUSEMAN gets up again and returns to speak to GASMAN.

Er . . . Hallo! . . . Er, it occurred to me you might like a cup of coffee.

GASMAN: (We're off already are we?) Wouldn't say no. Can't use the cooker though. I've 'ad to turn off your stop-cock. (You leering sod.)

HOUSEMAN: Oh. That's all right. I'll use the electric kettle.

> HOUSEMAN fills kettle and plugs it in.

(Why does it happen to me? It's not fair. Other people get funny old men in baggy overalls. I have to get beautiful boys in skintight jeans. It's not fair. It's just not fair.) How long have you been doing this job?

GASMAN: Couple of years.

HOUSEMAN: Do you like it?

GASMAN: It's okay. Nothing to write 'ome about. The money's good. I'm not complaining.

HOUSEMAN: Do you always wear jeans to work in? (Damn! Why did I ask him that? I must be more careful.)

GASMAN: (And we're over the first!) Well, they're practical—and they're cheap.

HOUSEMAN: (Laughs) I don't think that's the only reason people wear them. (As if you didn't know how well they show off your pretty little arse.)

GASMAN: What other reason would there be? (I knew it! I bleeding knew it!)

HOUSEMAN: (Are you really as naive as you seem? Or are you just fishing for compliments?) Well, some young men I know wear them because they think it makes them look . . . sexy.

GASMAN: (Laughs) (Was I right, or was I wrong?) If you're feeling sexy, it's a matter of taking things off, not putting them on, i'n'it?

HOUSEMAN: (Laughs) Yes. (And very lovely you'd look too, with nothing on. You're flirting with me, you little bastard, (Kettle boils) and I'd bet you'd bloody soon thump me one if I tried anything. Anyway, I don't fancy you that much, so in a minute I'm going to leave you all alone with your coffee and go and get on with my work.)

GASMAN: Your kettle's boiling.

HOUSEMAN: What?

GASMAN: Your water—it's boiling.

HOUSEMAN: Oh the water. Yes. Thanks.

      HOUSEMAN prepares cups, makes coffee etc.

GASMAN: (Funny. 'E seems to 'ave gone all quiet. Poor old bloke. I bet 'e's really lonely. I wouldn't change places with you matey—not even with all your money. Probably chatting up is as far as you ever go. Don't suppose you've ever made it to bed with ANYONE, 'ave you? And you really fancy me, don't yer?) So . . . er . . . you reckon it makes me look sexy, do yer?

HOUSEMAN: I didn't say that. I said OTHER people . . .

GASMAN: Fellers are always making passes at me. I dunno why.

HOUSEMAN: I wonder why that could be . . .

GASMAN: Wha'd'yer mean? I don't encourage no one. (But I wonder what it would be like. Just once. Just for the 'ell of it. It's all part of life's rich mosaic pattern, after all.)

HOUSEMAN: Some people might find your manner of dress provocative.

GASMAN: I'm only wearing a pair of old jeans, for Chrissake!

HOUSEMAN: (And the fact that they're so tight that you must've been melted down and poured into them is purely coincidental, I suppose.) How do you like your coffee?

GASMAN: In a cup.

HOUSEMAN: I mean what do you want in it?

GASMAN: Oh the usual things. Arsenic. LSD. What yer got?

HOUSEMAN: I've got sugar and milk.

GASMAN: Yeah, well I'll 'ave both them. (Lost interest, 'ave yer? Your trouble is that you obviously don't fancy yer chances 'alf enough. Pity. I reckon I could 'ave a go with you. You're certainly not what they'd call repulsive.)

HOUSEMAN pours milk, picks up sugar bowl and taps it.

GASMAN: Two. There, that's done. Shouldn't 'ave no more trouble with that. Just needed a spot of grease up yer flexible 'ose.

HOUSEMAN: Oh. Thanks. Here's your coffee.

GASMAN: Ta.

HOUSEMAN takes his own coffee and returns to other room.

HOUSEMAN: (I wonder what you'd be like if one really got to know you well. Do you ever wonder what life is about? Do you ever give even a moment's thought to death? What goes on inside that pretty little head of yours?)

GASMAN: (No time like the present, as they say. I'll give it a go.) Nice place you've got 'ere. Is that a colour telly?

HOUSEMAN: Yes, it is. I don't know why I have it really, the amount I watch.

59

GASMAN: ('Ere goes) I've never seen a colour telly working.

HOUSEMAN: Well I'm afraid you're out of luck. There's never anything much on at this time of day.

GASMAN: ('E 'asn't twigged.) Lovely programmes in the evenings, though, aren't there? In the EVENINGS.

HOUSEMAN: Yes. Quite often there are. (Why I do believe he's making advances!)

There is a pause. They look at each other.

GASMAN: (Poor old sod. 'E just can't get it together. Anyway, I don't fancy 'im that much. Just that it could've been, well, interesting.) Well, I must be pushing off. Another lovely young 'ousewife is awaiting my services somewhere. Just sign 'ere.

HOUSEMAN: (Signing) Thank you for going the job so quickly. There's a very good film on BBC2 tomorrow evening, actually. If you're interested.

GASMAN: You don't say. Well, I might just pop in and watch it with you then.

HOUSEMAN opens door. GASMAN goes through it.

Keep smiling. Cause you're not so bad-looking yerself. You know . . . See yer!

GASMAN exits and both men remain stationary on either side of the door as the lights slowly fade.

TEA

TUBEWOMAN: Suburban/smart/ordinary/30ish
HOUSEMAN: As before

A tube station. A train is heard entering the station and stopping. The doors open. Enter TUBEWOMAN. She stops to look at a poster. She speaks to it. As she speaks, she fumbles in her handbag for a felt pen and begins to deface the poster.

TUBEWOMAN: Ah you think you're so clever, don't you? You think you've really got it made, don't you? You think you know it all . . . With your soft, manageable hair and your creamy smooth complexion. You think you're so bloody clever, don't you? Eat it up. Drink it down. Put it on. Buy this. Buy that. Well let me tell you, you'll get your lot. Oh yes. Mark my words. You'll get your bloody lot one day. You're all bastards. The bloody lot of you. Bastards! Bastards! Bastards!

TUBEWOMAN sinks to the ground crying heavily, heaving with sobs and muttering incoherently. Enter HOUSEMAN. He walks past her, then stops, looks back, hesitates, comes back, looks, crouches down and speaks softly.

HOUSEMAN: Are you all right?

TUBEWOMAN: No. I'm not. I don't know . . . what to do.

HOUSEMAN: Do you need help?

TUBEWOMAN: (Desperately) Oh yes, please.

HOUSEMAN: Would you like to come and have a cup of tea with me? I live very near here.

TUBEWOMAN: (Desperately) Oh yes, please. But I don't think I can walk . . .

HOUSEMAN: Here, let me help you.

He helps her to her feet and together they go out into the street.

TUBEWOMAN: It's being underground that does it. I should've known better. It's claustrophobia, you see. People don't understand. I feel better already, out in the open air.

HOUSEMAN: Have you had it before?

TUBEWOMAN: Oh yes. Lots and lots of times.

HOUSEMAN: I see. Here we are. This is my door.

They enter HOUSEMAN's flat.

TUBEWOMAN: Isn't this nice? I never would've imagined this.

HOUSEMAN: Right. I'll go and put the kettle on.

TUBEWOMAN: I must look dreadful. Whatever must you have thought of me, lying on the ground, crying like a baby?

HOUSEMAN: I just thought you needed help.

TUBEWOMAN: Hmmmph! More than those other swine. Just walking right past me as if I didn't exist. Well . . . I'll go and do my face and then I'll feel fit to face the world again. Do you have a loo I could use?

HOUSEMAN: Yes. It's through there.

TUBEWOMAN goes to bathroom, takes a compact, lipstick etc. from her handbag, does her make-up, arranges her hair. Puts on a 'face'. HOUSEMAN makes tea and brings it on a tray.

HOUSEMAN: Ah, there you are. Do you take sugar and milk in your tea?

TUBEWOMAN: What must you think of me? I'm so sorry. I don't know what came over me.

HOUSEMAN: That's all right. You're looking much better now, anyway. Do you take sugar and milk in your tea?

TUBEWOMAN: Milk, but not sugar, please.

HOUSEMAN: Here you are.

      There is a pause. They drink their tea.

HOUSEMAN: Have you ever thought of going by bus, if the underground worries you so much?

TUBEWOMAN: Oh I can't stand being down there. I get this feeling of being shut in with no escape and then I panic. I know I shouldn't go down there, but it really is the most convenient way for me to get to work. And then, if I go by bus, it means I have this long walk to the stop and sometimes, well quite often really, I get this funny feeling that the pavement is going to start moving up and down and throw me off and then I can't walk properly and I begin to panic and I have to sit down, wherever I am, and then people start staring at me—as if they wanted to murder me. Well, they do that on the underground too, of course. Yes, that's true. In fact, everywhere I go people stare and stare and want to murder me and one day I'm going to get myself a machine-gun and shoot them all. Do YOU ever feel you could shoot everyone in the world?

HOUSEMAN: Er . . . No. I can't say that I do.

TUBEWOMAN: My mother said that I . . . But I mustn't talk so much. I MUST NOT talk so much.

HOUSEMAN: You can talk as much as you want to. What's in the bag?

TUBEWOMAN: Oh it's a pullover. I just bought it in a sale. It was a bargain if I do say so myself, not that I think you're the kind to contradict me.

HOUSEMAN: No.

TUBEWOMAN: It's pure cashmere.

HOUSEMAN: Can I see it?

TUBEWOMAN: Of course. It's blue you see. I always buy blue. Don't you think this blue suits me? Now my mother wanted me to get a

63

green one. But I hate green. Pooh! She never lets me wear blue.
She always wants to tell me what to do—to tell ME what's good
for HER. She won't ever let me do just what I want. I tell her, I
mean I say to her, 'Look, mother, I'm over thirty now and women
of thirty just don't do what their mothers say . . .' But she still
goes on and on about it until I could murder. I could easily
murder HER. I expect I will one day. She makes me go to parties.
I stand in the room. All those people. And I feel shut in, no
escape, and then I panic and I want to machine-gun them all
down. You must have felt that, haven't you? Everyone feels that,
don't they? From time to time, I mean. Everyone wishes that she
could have a gun and go into a crowded room and just go bam
bam bam bam bam bam bam bam bam bam bam. All dead! Ha!
Ha! Then they'd be sorry! Then perhaps they'd leave me alone.
Are you a photographer?

HOUSEMAN: Sorry?

TUBEWOMAN: I said, 'Are you a photographer?' ARE . . . YOU . . .
A . . . PHOTOGRAPHER? I mean you're so good-looking and you
have this beautiful flat. I just thought you must be a
photographer. Not that I can see any photographs anywhere, but I
just thought, like that, you know.

HOUSEMAN: Well, I can't see that it follows from any of the things
you've said. But, yes, as a matter of fact, I am.

TUBEWOMAN: I thought so. I'm very perceptive, you see. My mother
always did admit that . . .
'You're very perceptive, you little bitch.'
She was always calling me a bitch. And I bet you have lots and lots
of really beautiful women coming after you. So you'd never want
to know a dowdy old wreck like me. I mean why should you be
interested in someone my age? So there's no need for me to
bother thinking in THAT direction, is there? No need at all.
Thinking can be such a bother, can't it? Did you see that film
called 'BLOW UP'? That was about this handsome young
photographer and these two girls went to his studio to try and get
some work and they got something else. Oh my goodness me, they
got something quite different. Have YOU ever raped anyone?

HOUSEMAN: Now, let's get something straight. In the first place you are not a dowdy old wreck. In fact you're very attractive and you know it. And in the second place, I am basically gay.

TUBEWOMAN: Gay? What does that mean?

HOUSEMAN: It means homosexual. It means I prefer MEN to women, sexually. So you see, you have nothing to fear.

TUBEWOMAN: How marvellous! How marvellous! Now my mother would have said I was wrong to come here. She definitely would have said so.

> From this point on, when TUBEWOMAN speaks her mother's lines, she BECOMES her mother.

'You're never to go into strange men's houses. They all want the same thing, and it's our job to make sure that they don't get it.'
'But mother, how am I ever to meet the man I'm going to marry?'
'You'll marry when I'M good and ready, not before, my girl. There's only one fate for girls who go into strange men's houses. I'm not having a daughter of mine ending up like that . . .'
'But mother, I'm quite old enough to look after myself.'
'Old enough! You're just a child. That's all. Just a child.'

Do you ever have orgies here?

HOUSEMAN: What?

TUBEWOMAN: Orge-eez?

HOUSEMAN: No. I have a very long-standing relationship with a man I love very much. It keeps me happy. I don't need anything more.

TUBEWOMAN: Lucky! Lucky you! Now ME—I'm all alone in this whole rotten world. I haven't even got anywhere to sleep tonight! Can you imagine that? I don't even know where I'm going to SLEEP tonight!

HOUSEMAN: Are you telling me that you haven't got a home to go to?

TUBEWOMAN: Not that I want you to think that I would like to stay HERE. Oh no! It would never even occur to me to ask you. You've already been very kind. I expect you're very busy and have lots of photographs to take.

She stands up and helps herself to more tea.

In fact I was just leaving. Well in a moment. Well perhaps I'll stay a few moments more. How kind of you to ask me. Not at all, you're very welcome.

She sits down again.

TUBEWOMAN: I wonder if you're completely . . . gay. My mother was no fool and she told me to be very careful. And I always take my mother's advice in absolutely everything.
'They're up to all sorts of tricks to catch us out. They'll lie and cheat. They'll pretend to be gay.'
'Yes, mother.'
'We women must stand firm. He's very good-looking I know, but you must leave now. You're in great danger.'
'Yes, mother.'

HOUSEMAN: I can assure you you are in no danger. If you have no home, why haven't you got any luggage with you?

TUBEWOMAN: Everything I own in the whole world is in this carrier bag.

HOUSEMAN: But you said you just bought that pullover in a sale.

TUBEWOMAN: So I did. So I did. But that was ages ago. Last year I think.

HOUSEMAN: What about your mother? You were talking about your mother. Can't you go there?

TUBEWOMAN: She's dead. She died years and years ago. I can hardly remember her. Oh, she was a good mother to me and now she's gone and I'm all alone in the world. Mind you, she still talks to me. But it's not the same. Sometimes I think I'll buy a net and go out and catch someone and take them home and keep them and then I won't be lonely any more. Did you see a film called 'THE COLLECTOR'?

HOUSEMAN: No, I didn't. Now listen. I'm sorry you're so lonely. And I'm sorry I can't help you. But I'm going to have to leave in a minute—I'm going . . .

TUBEWOMAN: (Interrupting him) I'm going. I'm going. Right now. Thank you for being so kind to me. I feel better. Really I do. Perhaps I could come and visit you sometimes. You're so good-looking. But no. What would you want with an old hag like me around. You don't need anyone you said. You have your boyfriend, or whatever you called him. Lucky! Now where did I put my handbag? I can't have lost it! Oh no! It's got all my keys in it. Oh I know! I left it in the loo. I won't be a minute.

HOUSEMAN: I was going to say, that I'm going to the theatre and I've arranged to meet Jimmy outside and I've got the tickets, so he can't get in without me. Otherwise I wouldn't ask you to leave. And do please come and talk to me again—if you'd like to.

> She reaches out as if to touch him, but doesn't.

TUBEWOMAN: Don't worry. I understand perfectly. I'll just use your loo again though, if I may. The tea you know—goes through so quickly. (Laughs)

> TUBEWOMAN exits to bathrom. HOUSEMAN goes to telephone, dials number. During the following telephone conversation, we see TUBEWOMAN take out a soft object from her handbag and nurse it, while sucking her thumb. (During the original production, she used a piece of old blanket)

HOUSEMAN: Hallo, Jimmy.
   (PAUSE)
No. No. I've got them. I'll meet you in the foyer as arranged. No. I'm ringing about something else. As I was coming out of the underground station, I saw this poor woman lying on the ground, crying and sobbing. She was in a terrible state and everyone was just walking past her. I mean, some people were actually stepping over her as if she . . .
   (PAUSE)
Well, anyway, I . . .
   (PAUSE)
Yes, but Jimmy, that's not the point. The point is, she's still here. She's about to leave and I don't know what to do.
   (PAUSE)
But, Jimmy, she seems to be completely mad. I don't know if I

ought to let her just walk off into the night . . .
(PAUSE)
She says she hasn't.
(PAUSE)
In the loo. She's got her handbag with her. I think she probably has got somewhere to go to, despite what she says, because she's clean and well-dressed and she's only got a carrier bag with her with a brand-new pullover in it. Also, it's true, she just said something about her keys . . .
(PAUSE)
Yes. So I'll meet you in the foyer as arranged then. In about twenty minutes.

TUBEWOMAN re-enters from bathroom.

Mmmm. Me too. Bye.

TUBEWOMAN: Was that your boy-friend?

HOUSEMAN: Yes.

TUBEWOMAN: Well, I'm just off

HOUSEMAN: You look a lot better. I hope you'll be more careful in the future.

TUBEWOMAN: More careful?

HOUSEMAN: About going down the underground. Have you ever thought of going to see a doctor about your . . . claustrophobia?

TUBEWOMAN: Oh yes. Of course. I've seen hundreds of doctors. Well, thank you so much for the tea. It's been a real pleasure meeting you. I do so hope we'll meet again someday. And I hope you enjoy your visit to the theatre.

HOUSEMAN: And you think you'll be all right . . . out there?

TUBEWOMAN: All right? Of course. You have been very kind. Goodbye.

TUBEWOMAN turns and walks off into the audience. HOUSEMAN stares after her for a moment, then goes to a chair and sits down with a sigh as the lights slowly fade.

68

WINE

MICHAEL: Scruffy/grubby (not filthy)/charismatic/Irish/
40ish
DIM: Scruffy/filthy/surly/sullen/Cockney/age unknown
STREAKY: Scruffy/coughs & sniffles/asleep throughout/age
unknown
GASMAN: As before
TUBEWOMAN: As before
ROGER: Gentle/self-composed/quiet/Gay Freak/Jesus look

A park. Birdsong. MICHAEL, DIM & STREAKY are
occupying a bench as if it were a mansion. STREAKY is in
the middle and is asleep. As the lights come up, MICHAEL is
draining the last possible drop from a wine bottle. He holds it
upside down to make sure there is really nothing left in it.

MICHAEL: In my beginning is my end.

He places the empty bottle on the ground beside the bench
with exaggerated care.

DIM: That one's ended, anyway.

Using his own cider bottle, DIM repeats MICHAEL's
actions.

And mine too. Done. Finished. Over.

MICHAEL: It's back in the hands of providence we are. Here comes
someone . . .

Enter GASMAN. He walks across, determinedly not seeing
the three men on the bench. MICHAEL tries to attract his
attention.

MICHAEL: Good evening to you, sir! I wonder if . . .

But GASMAN has ignored him. MICHAEL gives him a
two-finger farewell. As GASMAN exits, he encounters
TUBEWOMAN entering. They look at each other as they
pass.

69

DIM: Stopped. Con-clude-dead. Played out.

MICHAEL: (Seeing TUBEWOMAN) Ah, this looks more likely.

> MICHAEL gets up and accosts her.

Good evening to you, madam. I wonder if you could spare a few pence for a bite to eat and a cup of tea?

TUBEWOMAN: No. You'd only spend it on more drink. I know your sort.

> She stares at DIM.

DIM: Drawwwwwn to a close.

> TUBEWOMAN tries to walk off, but MICHAEL persists.

MICHAEL: Sure and there's no alcoholic drink can be bought for the price of a cup of tea, lady. Not according to my knowledge of this holy city, anyway.

> TUBEWOMAN begins fumbling with her handbag. She is going to give in.

Bless you madam. You'll never want for a friend when you have a heart of gold, they say.

TUBEWOMAN: Here you are then. But don't spend it on more drink, mind.

MICHAEL: Ah, thank you, lady. Sure I swear it on the holy book itself.

> TUBEWOMAN exits. DIM points at her receding back.

DIM: Excited. Passed away. Gone off.

MICHAEL: Want to buy your soul for a few pence, they do. And the likes of us not even allowed NEAR the off-licence, anyway.

DIM: Ceased. Come to a stand-still. Halted.

He looks at MICHAEL.

I have stomach-ache.

MICHAEL sits down again.

MICHAEL: (Irony) What a beautiful magic day we've had today! How will it all end, I wonder?

MICHAEL looks at DIM. There is a pause.

DIM: You're losing your touch.

MICHAEL: And wouldn't that be apelike if it were true! And me a Leo! Expect nothing and you can suffer no disappointment.

DIM: Is it better to lose it, meaning I suppose that you must have had it once. Or is it better never to have had it in the first place. Like me. Good. Better. Best.

MICHAEL: There is nothing either good or bad, but thinking makes it so.

MICHAEL stands up and bows extravagantly.

I'm forever honouring your memory and your name, you darling wonderful man.

He sits down again.

God. But I had a powerful great dream last night! Powerful!

DIM: I've had a terrible thought these last days. Plagueing me. Jesus! Terrible!

MICHAEL: Out with it! Thoughts have no place in that dark void you call a mind. Tell me the thought and I'll tell you my demon dream.

DIM: Fearful. Horrible. Ghaaastly.

MICHAEL: Will you listen to the man? Tell me the thought and I'll tell you my dream.

71

DIM: Serious, though, Michael.

MICHAEL: It's serious he wants me to be. And it's serious I always am. As he knows full well. Especially when I'm joking. Wait. Holy Mary, Mother of God! Will you look what's coming! It's HIMSELF, coming to provide for us!

> Enter ROGER. He is carrying a bottle of wine and a loaf of bread. He smiles at MICHAEL & DIM. MICHAEL's mouth drops open. ROGER exits. MICHAEL recovers his senses.

MICHAEL: Friend . . . Please . . . Just . . .

> Michael gets up to go after ROGER, but the latter has heard him and turned back anyway. They meet at the side.

We were wondering if you'd be after letting us share in your good fortune, friend.

ROGER: This? I'm on my way to a party and my friends asked me to bring a bottle.

MICHAEL: Ah! Just a drop. They'll never notice.

ROGER: Here. Have it. Why not? I can easily get some more on the way.

> MICHAEL reaches out to take the bottle, but looks disbelieving.

Go on. It's yours.

> MICHAEL takes the bottle. ROGER makes as if to leave.

MICHAEL: Bless you, my friend. But will you not sit with us and share?

> ROGER is genuinely surprised and happy at this invitation.

ROGER: Thank you. I'd like to.

> This involves moving STREAKY to the side so that ROGER can sit between MICHAEL and DIM. STREAKY doesn't

wake during this procedure, though he coughs and sniffles a bit. ROGER breaks pieces off the bread and offers them to the others. DIM stares at his piece, doesn't eat it, puts it on STREAKY's lap instead. MICHAEL opens the wine bottle and toasts the world.

MICHAEL: Bless everyone who can smile and sustain everyone who cannot!

MICHAEL drinks and passes the bottle to ROGER who drinks in silence and passes it on to DIM. DIM doesn't drink, but in a continuous movement, the bottle passes from him to STREAKY, who awakes as if by magic, drinks, coughs, splutters, drinks, until DIM snatches the bottle away from him again. DIM passes the bottle back to ROGER, again without drinking.

ROGER: Don't you want any?

DIM: Not my drink.

ROGER passes the bottle back to MICHAEL.

MICHAEL: Sure my friend there will drink nothing but cider. But for you and me, wine is the only fitting drink, I'm thinking.

MICHAEL drinks again.

DIM: Useless drinking wine. Takes you up. Brings you down. Pointless.

ROGER: Is there an off-licence anywhere around?

MICHAEL: Indeed there is. And 'tis a miserable lot of humanity inhabits it. They call the police if we so much as go near the place.

ROGER stands up.

Are you leaving us so soon, friend?

ROGER: No. I'll be back. But could you tell me where the off-licence is, please?

MICHAEL: Sure and I'll walk with you and show you, if I may.

>   MICHAEL puts his wine bottle down with extreme care.
>   Points his finger at it, speaks to it.

Stay there.

>   He gets up and he and ROGER exit together.

*DIM: I'LL be back.
I'LL walk with you and show you.
If I may.
I.
Makes no sense.
He thinks it does. He thinks everything does. So why will he not
realise that it's serious? Important. Cardinal. Grave. Yes, that's it.
Grave. Streaky, listen.

>   He shakes STREAKY who coughs and splutters but doesn't
>   open his eyes.

Listen. When I say 'I' and 'me', what do I mean? Who am I? What
am I? How can I ever know? HOW?

>   He waits, but STREAKY is not going to answer.

Did you hear my question?

>   He shakes STREAKY again.

DIM: (Shouting) Dd you hear my question?

STREAKY: What? Did a person speak?

>   Re-enter MICHAEL, singing.

MICHAEL: Oh what a beautiful evening!
Oh what a beautiful day!
I've got a wonderful feeling

>   MICHAEL punches DIM on the shoulder.

Something is coming our way.

> MICHAEL sits down again.

Are you not sometimes overcome with admiration for the wonderful mystery it all is?

DIM: What?

MICHAEL: Life.

DIM: I've got stomach-ache.

MICHAEL: Well don't you go worrying about that, Dim, my lad. That lovely boy has gone to get some soothing nectar for your poor abused gut. And for him and me, there's still all this.

> He picks up the wine bottle and holds it up to the light.

Ripened in the sunlight. Matured in the darkness. Like my poor mortal soul.

DIM: Eh?

MICHAEL: Wine, Dim, wine. The gift of holy truth from compassionate gods to lonely, suffering, LYING mortals, like ourselves.

DIM: I only drink cider.

MICHAEL: Holy Mother! He's getting you some. Have I not been telling you these past five minutes? He's getting you some.

DIM: I love you.

> MICHAEL puts his arm round STREAKY and pulls him into a hug.

MICHAEL: And I love you too, you silly old heap of a man. Listen, tell me your serious thought, and I'll, tell you my demon dream.

DIM: Grave. Not serious. Grave.

MICHAEL: So, tell it to me.

DIM: It's grave.

MICHAEL: Grave then.

> MICHAEL pushes DIM away from him.

> And aren't you becoming the perfect little pedant?

DIM: Well, see, it's like this . . . I . . .

MICHAEL: (Interrupting) Ah! Here's our fine new friend, back again!

> Re-enter ROGER. He has another bottle of wine and a bottle of cider. He offers the cider to DIM.

ROGER: Here. This is for you.

> DIM takes the bottle and nods but doesn't speak.

ROGER: You did say it was cider you liked, didn't you?

> DIM nods again. MICHAEL speaks for him.

MICHAEL: Bless you. You're a lovely lad.

ROGER: May I sit with you a little while longer?

MICHAEL: Indeed you may. We were hoping you would.

> ROGER sits down between MICHAEL and DIM again. DIM opens the bottle of cider and drinks from it as if it were a baby's bottle. He keeps the cap in his other hand.

ROGER: I'm Roger. Could you tell me your names, please?

MICHAEL: Well, Roger, the sleeper at the end is Streaky.

DIM: Dim.

> STREAKY coughs and splutters.

MICHAEL: And I'm Michael.

ROGER: Is Streaky all right?

MICHAEL: Oh, he's sound, Roger. He's sound. Never better. Beautiful clear speech you have. A joy to hear it. Are you a literary man? You have the eyes of a literary man.

ROGER: I write stuff. Yes. But I wouldn't call it literary.

MICAHEL: Stick to it. Sure if we'll only let them, the gods will speak through us.

MICHAEL points at ROGER's GLF badge.

What's that?

ROGER: It's a GLF badge.

MICHAEL: GLF, Roger. What is that?

ROGER: Gay Liberation Front. It's a movement for the liberation of homosexuals.

DIM: Homosexuals. Liberation.

MICHAEL stands up.

MICHAEL: Give me your hand! A child of the future age, at last!

ROGER stands up and he and MICHAEL shake hands. MICHAEL keeps hold of him.

Ah! T'is good to meet an honest man!

ROGER: I'm just the same as everyone else, you know.

MICHAEL: I knew Brendan Behan. He was like you. But not honest about it. Ah, 't'is fine honest eyes you have.

ROGER gently pulls his hand away and sits down again.

ROGER: Thank you. What did you mean by 'child of the future age'?

MICHAEL: Ah, that's William Blake, Roger. A glorious genius of the English language.

> MICHAEL sits down again.

Listen:
Children of the Future Age
Reading this indignant page,
Know that in a former time
Love! sweet Love!
Was thought a crime.

DIM: Dear Mother!

> DIM stands up. He is going to recite.

Dear Mother, the Church is cold,
But the Ale-House is healthy and pleasant and warm;
Besides I can tell where I am used well,
Such usage in heaven will never do well.

But if at the Church they would give us some Ale,
And a pleasant fire our souls to regale,
We'd sing and we'd pray all the live-long day,
Nor ever once wish from the Church to stray.

MICHAEL: Bravo, Dim!

DIM: Except that I don't like Ale.

> DIM sits down again.

MICHAEL: Tell me, Roger, what is it like for a man, to love a man?

ROGER: What is it like for anyone to love anyone?

MICHAEL: Ah. And have you loved many?

ROGER: (Smiling) I've had my fair share.

MICHAEL: I loved a woman once. Oh, just so much.

He indicates an inch with his thumb and forefinger.

But she loved someone else. And it was so painful to me that I had to leave. I couldn't be even in the same country as her. 'T'was then I went on the road.

DIM: On the road. Under way. Pushing on.

ROGER: What's it like, being on the road? Have you ever regretted it?

MICHAEL: Never once. I've loved every minute of my life. Sure, regret is wasted energy.

DIM: Everything is wasted energy. Getting ahead. Overtaking.

ROGER: (To MICHAEL) May I see your palms?

MICHAEL: Do you read palms, Roger?

ROGER: Oh, only in an amateur sort of way. But I enjoy doing it. And it's a good excuse for holding hands with people.

ROGER's head is bent as he examines MICHAEL's palms. MICHAEL looks down at his bent head with warmth—it could almost be love.

DIM: Out in front. Ah! Alone!

ROGER: It's a good strong hand with a sense of purpose.

He looks up into MICHAEL's eyes.

Like your eyes. Clear. Bright. They're very beautiful. I can see you've lived well.

MICHAEL leans forward and kisses ROGER on the lips. ROGER doesn't withdraw or participate exactly, but he puts his arm on MICHAEL's shoulder. When MICHAEL pulls back, ROGER smiles. ROGER turns to DIM.

ROGER: May I see your palm, Dim? ·

DIM offers it without expression. It still has the cider cap in it. ROGER takes the cider cap from DIM's palm and puts it on the bench beside him. MICHAEL sits back and stares ahead. He seems dazed.

MICHAEL: Brendan always wanted that from me. And me wondering all these years what it would be like. And I suppose wanting it too in a way. Ah, but somehow we never made it happen. Ah, Roger, you've given me something to think about there.

ROGER looks up at the sound of his name.

DIM: What can you see?

ROGER: (Looking at DIM's palm) Why do you hate yourself so much? You're no different from anyone else you know. But you don't even take care of your body.

He looks up into DIM's eyes.

If you won't love yourself, how can anyone else?

DIM snatches his hand away.

DIM: I only like cider. He drinks wine. Not me.

ROGER: Cider's okay. But try and eat something sometimes too.

MICHAEL: Ah! You're right there, Roger, indeed you are. I long ago gave up trying. Stubborn as a teetotal bishop, he is.

DIM: It's my way. My way. Mine.

MICHAEL & DIM glare at each other across ROGER. ROGER stands up.

MICHAEL: Are you leaving us, Roger?

ROGER: I want to go to my party now. My friends are giving it in my honour.

MICHAEL: Then a final toast before you leave.

MICHAEL stands up, turns his back on the audience and
toasts the cast.

I drink to the few honest souls in this dishonest city.

He drinks, then offers the bottle to ROGER who also drinks,
then hands the bottle back to MICHAEL. ROGER tries to
shake hands with DIM, who at first refuses, but finally agrees.
ROGER touches STREAKY on the shoulder, thereby
producing some mild spluttering. He turns to say goodbye to
MICHAEL.

MICHAEL: Will you come and sit with us again?

ROGER: I'd like to. But I'm going abroad tomorrow for a few months.
That's what the party's for—saying goodbye.

MICHAEL: Then, farewell, Roger.

MICHAEL and ROGER shake hands and ROGER gives
MICHAEL a light kiss on the lips. As ROGER exits,
MICHAEL calls after him:

MICHAEL: God be with you!

MICHAEL sits down again.

Ah Damn! It's the likes of me that'll be the ruination of the world.
I meant to tell him my wonderful dream—and I forgot! Would you
be after believing that? I FORGOT.

He holds up the wine bottle and speaks to it.

Sure, it'll take all your skill to console me, and you feeling weak
and poorly yourself, now.

DIM: Tell me.

MICHAEL: What?

DIM: Tell me your dream.

MICHAEL: All right so. If you'll tell me your 'grave' thought.

DIM: Streaky must be in the middle.

> MICHAEL thinks this is daft, but agrees. They rearrange
> themselves as at the beginning. MICHAEL waits for calm.

MICHAEL: I'm on . . . an impossible journey. There's a deep well and,
somehow, I've contrived a sort of rope, attached at the top and
wrapped in a curious way around my middle—so that I can feed it
out as I need it. I'm going to lower myself down this well—(laughs)
and me always terrified of heights! At first, as I begin to go down,
hand over hand, I can feel the solid walls in the darkness. When I
reach up to test the rope, I see it glowing like a silver thread in the
black tunnel of the well . . . At last, I'm at the bottom. I want to
explore, but I find myself quaking with fear. What if the rope
comes loose at the top? What if the rope breaks? What if I find
myself wanting in strength to climb up again? I reach my arms out
into the blackness till they're stretched to their limits. Everywhere
I reach, there's nothing. Nothing at all. As I reach into it, it seems
to push back at me, this . . . NOTHINGNESS. It's almost like a
kind of physical presence. I can feel it beginning to stifle me. I'm
suffocating! I can't breathe! I'm going to DIE!!! And then it hits
me that THAT IS THE ANSWER! There is absolutely nothing at
the bottom of this famous well! It's a vision of the holy grail! And
me always searching, searching! There is no well. There is no rope.
There is no up and no down. Why, there isn't even a 'me' to climb!
Suddenly I'm filled with a powerful joy and with a final vast
effort, I cry aloud: 'I've found it! I can perform miracles! Me! I
can create a universe!' . . . And there I am, startled awake, and the
sky with a million stars above my head. And the moon shining
down on me, like it knew all the time.

DIM: There's nothing. Nothing. That's my fear, exactly. Terror. That
was my thought, exactly.

> MICHAEL leaps to his feet with impatience.

MICHAEL: No, no, no. Joy, not terror. We are alive. The world exists
because we are making it all the time. We! Out of nothing. And
we can make it any way we like. Daily magic. Wake. Look at the
sky, the sun, the clouds. Wonder at it! Love it! Ah, here's to you,
Roger, and all the honest souls like you.

> He turns and toasts the audience.

And here's to you all. CHILDREN OF THE FUTURE AGE.   82

'THE HAUNTED HOST'
by Robert Patrick

The first performance in the United Kingdom of 'The Haunted Host'
was at Inter-Action's Almost Free Theatre, Rupert Street, London W1,
on Monday, 19th May, 1974, with the following cast:

Jay: Joseph Pichette
Frank: Ned Van Zandt

An Inter-Action Production designed by Norman Coates and directed
by John Chapman

Approximate playing time: 1 hour 50 minutes

All rights whatsoever in this Play are strictly reserved and applications
for performance, both amateur and professional, in the United
Kingdom shall be made to:
Fraser and Dunlop (Scripts) Ltd.
91 Regent Street
London W1R 8RU
No performance or use of the Play may be made unless a licence has
been obtained prior to rehearsal.

The setting is the living room of JAY's apartment. It is situated just above the main homosexual cruising crossroads, Christopher St. and Greenwich Ave. in Manhattan. There is a door to the hallway, another to the remainder of the paratment, and a window overlooking the intersection. The apartment, itself is tacky as hell, littered, dirty, but not stagnant. It is apparent that whoever lives here is always on the go, although the appearance would suggest that he is going in a circle. Mostly there are clothes tossed around, magazines and books, dozens upon dozens of cigarette packages. On a desk is a huge, dirty, ragged stack of papers, tied into a bundle with cord. These are the writings of Ed, the ghost. A large photo of Ed hangs over the couch. He was a handsome young man, just short of classically beautiful.

> At rise, JAY, the host, is kicking around the apartment looking very nervous indeed. JAY is a few years older than Ed looks in the picture. HE is energetic, flamboyant, dazzling in the personality department when he wants to be, and his gesture and expression suggest intelligence. HE is not very handsome, and his manner of dress—which suggests he has just walked through somebody's wet wash—is not designed to enhance whatever attractive features he might have. HE holds a rolled-up poster in his hands, and keeps casting guilty looks at the photo of Ed, and at a spot in the air which contains Ed's ghost. Finally, in a mad burst of organized energy, HE takes down the photo and affixes to the wall the ugliest Kandinsky print ever remaindered at Marboro Book Shops.

JAY: (To Ghost) There! (Mock Bette Davis) Do you like it? (Serious, thumbing through papers on desk) Did you like any abstract art at all? Well, it's NOT my favourite picture—(Ironically) it's not even my favourite KIND of picture, but—(Defensively) it interested me! (Superior) Well, I know it bores YOU, but just possibly it might hold some kind of feeling or outlook, or whatever, that will come in valuable some time. Just BECAUSE it bores you, because it IS a strange way of feeling forced on you from outside—an emotion or attitude that you'd never feel, or never follow if you DID feel—a SHOCK!—just possibly it might help you get out of yourself for a minute. Because the things we like, even the people we like, are just ourselves, just—talking to ourselves. We have to get OUT . . . Because we need to, we have to. We live in such a crowd. (Mocking his own melodramatics) We ARE such a crowd, every one of us; so much of us is other people that have come at us all our lives like—COOKIE CUTTERS!—that only some constant kind of openness, availability, can let in enough ideas to help us even begin to determine who in Hell we are. Who on EARTH we are. Who in HEAVEN we are! (Smugly pleased with this phrase, but trying to conceal it) Oh, for Christ's sake, baby—don't admire my phrases— (Mock-pedantic) check my premises! (Ghost speaks) I will call you "baby" as long as you act like one (Ghost speaks, JAY interrupts) Yes, yes, of course our personalities are formed by our experience—and that idea, by the way, is not yours, but Sigmund Freud's, it came to you from outside, touché!—but all that means is that we ARE shaped, we CAN be shaped. I know it's no fun to change, or even to try to see what you're really like, to TRY to change, but we can . . . What? (Ghost interrupts. JAY repeats his inquiry, mocking the Ghost's Southern accent) Do Ah buh-leeve that pee-pull evah really change? Of course, cookie! All we DO is change! Why, when you first started working for a living, when you first had sex—when you first started smoking, especially— didn't you change? Didn't your LIFE change, absolutely, every time? At least until you found a way to work the new prop, or the new character, into the same old inner drama! Or let some scientist come up with a new pill, or a new plastic, or a good oral contraceptive, or, please God, a psychology that works—or let some dumb damned politician pass a new law, and WATCH lives change! (HE fervently believes this, and is offended by the Ghost's quick reply) No, idiot, you can't change your feelings. I didn't say a word about feelings, get the spit out of your ears! (He becomes intensely serious) Listen, you can't change what you feel — but you can change what you do. Look at us. (Indicates messy room) You changed my life, I sure as hell changed yours. Only think—if we had known that we were going to. If we had decided to use each other for something good—

> The phone rings. HE is puzzled; it never rings. HE follows the phone cord and finds the phone deep in the wastebasket, under many papers. HE unwinds the phone from its cord, blows dust from it, and answers, cautiously.

Hello? (HE instantly snaps into a high-queenish character) Oh,

HELLO, Jo Wanda . . . No, I don't answer the phone funny anymore, it encourages people to call . . . How are you? How's that man you're living with? . . . And the one he's living with? . . . You sound it . . . Oh, I'M fine, I'm good for another ten years unless I do something quick . . . Oh, nothing, I was just going through Ed's papers. Why. What do you need? . . . A favour? A favour? How dare you ask me for a favour, after all the favours you've done for me, and ruin my winning streak? What is it? . . . Huh? (Looks around room, a little dazed) Uhh—sure! Sure he can stay here! I mean, if I can stay here, he can stay here Just point him at my side of the Village and tell him to COME ACROSS! What's he like? . . . (Laughs) No, you sex maniac, not what DOES he like; what IS he like? I don't care WHO he is, but WHAT is he? . . . Straight. Does he need a chaser? . . . No no no—I don't mind if he don't mind. Besides, I've already had your whole graduating class up here; I don't want to start on the underclassmen. I will put him in my living-bedroom. (Tests softness of sofa with his foot) . . . I have my own sheets, thank you! You are not sending that child out on the streets of Greenwich Village on Saturday night with an armload of bedclothes—not here in the overkill area where I live! (Peeks out window) Woo! Tell him to walk fast; the happy hunting grounds are infested tonight! You know, I live across from this little bakery—and all I can see are hot cross buns! Hurry the lamb over, I'll start some coffee. 'Bye. (But Jo Wanda will not be put off without his usual sisterly farewell) And a good buh-buh-ba-bye to you, too (Hangs up) Twit! (Looks at room with new eyes, quickly and capably arranges during his next lines some modicum of order). La la la la—another little visitor from the future! (To Ghost) Look, Jo Wanda is sending over some frat brother of yours and hers for me to entertain—so I would appreciate it if for once you would just behave like other people's ghosts and PLAY DEAD! (HE exits, toting laundry, before he can hear the Ghost's rejoinder. The phone begins to ring again. HE re-enters with a pile of bedclothes, stares at phone, tosses bedclothes on counch and answers) Hello? . . . Look, I just talked to you, don't monopolize . . . Well, there's always the chance somebody will dial a wrong number . . . On his way? Already? How are you sending him, by stork? . . . So what now? . . . Secrets! . . . He is? . . . Oh, he is . . . Large bore or small bore? . . . (Finishing Jo Wanda's sentence) And you want me to get him out of your hair . . . Oh, all the way out of New York, you've let your hair grow! . . . Well, consider it done! I will put the Dispose-All in gear. He will be back in Iowa for breakfast—which I will have on you, incidentally! . . . Ho-kay . . . Oh, by the way, let me know if you ever wanna get rid of Burt. (Sexy) No charge.

> During this, the GUEST appears at the door, having wandered down the hallway checking numbers. HE is the living image of Ed's picture. HE wears a grotesquely coloured collegiate letter-sweater, carries a suitcase and an overnight bag, and has a conspicuous script rolled up in his back pocket. HE rings. While waiting, HE polishes his shoes by rubbing each in turn on the back of his trouser legs.

Hold on, he's buzzing.

> JAY goes to downstairs-door speaker, buzzes it, shrieks into it, "Hello! Hello! Hello!" and returns to phone. The GUEST hears him approach door and readies a big smile, is baffled when the door does not open, and momentarily eavesdrops on the phone conversation inside, which HE cannot make out, before ringing again. HE should comb his hair quickly and carefully in the interim.

Now let me off the hook huh, I've got to mess the place up again before he climbs the stairs . . . A what? . . . A sur-what? . . . I don't want a surprise, sugar—I don't even want the inevitable! 'Bye! (Hangs up) Twat!

> GUEST rings the bell again.

Oh, Lord! (Yells) Just a minute! (Grabs some loose laundry and/or papers and litters the place again, runs over to a mirror and quickly ties his hair up in a ridiculous topknot or dons a mammoth string of beads. Surveys the effect. GUEST continues to ring, rather impatiently) Ring out the old, ring in the new! (To Ghost) Would this get rid of you? One hopes! (Instantly a little regretful, as he always is of unkindness to the Ghost) I'm sorry. (Dances like Bambi to the door, puts on his queeniest air) Ready or not! (Opens the door) Hell—(Does an enormous take at GUEST'S resemblance to Ed. Slams door)—Low! (Runs to grab Ed's photo, hides it behind sofa, looks at the mess, says, "Oh, fuck it!", takes hair down or beads off and zooms back to fling door open; looks back and forth from GUEST to Ghost, checking resemblance)

GUEST (Who has been caught checking door number against a slip of paper) Uh—hello?

JAY: (Whisks BOY in) Well, hello, come in, I'm your host! (Slams door and leans against it) And you're my parasite!

GUEST: (Standing, holding his luggage) Uh, you were expecting me, weren't you? I mean, you looked at me funny.

JAY: Well, I'm funny-looking. (These compulsive bad jokes usually cause JAY to be terribly polite afterwards) No no no, you look a great deal like someone. And I'm sure you are. Come on IN! (HE ushers GUEST further into room. Phone rings, JAY picks it up, answers without waiting for a "Hello") Hello, Jo Wanda. I was expecting you to phone about him, don't start anything you can't finish in Hell! (Hangs up three or four times noisily) Here, give me those!
>   Grabs GUEST's bags and stows them behind desk. GUEST follows right behind and extends his hand, so that JAY turns around to find it in his face.

GUEST: (Winning friends, influencing people) I'm Frank!

JAY: Ha! And don't I wish that everybody was! (Shakes hand) I'm Jay. Give coat. (Whips coat from GUEST) Sit down. (FRANK sits on couch. All this very quick) This is your bed. It unfolds into a nightmare! (HE is already exiting with FRANK's coat, which HE holds like an odoriferous dead animal)

FRANK: Ha! Is that out of your play?

JAY: (Surprised FRANK knows HE writes plays) Yes, completely out. Want some coffee? (HE exits)

FRANK: (Shouting) Black, no sugar!

JAY: (Off) I must jot that down!

FRANK (Shouting) I thought I heard—do you have somebody here?

JAY: (Re-entering with complete ill-assorted coffee service on tray) Not so much anymore, just the house ghosts. Why, is there anyone in particular you'd like?

FRANK: Uh, no—I thought I heard you talking to someone.

JAY: (Eyeing phone viciously. Coffee gets served somewhere in here) Yes, a former friend!

FRANK: (Delighted) Who, a ghost? (JAY drops spoon or something) You really believe in ghosts? John said you did.

JAY: I scarcely believe in anything else anymore. Do you?

FRANK: No, frankly, I don't.

JAY: How about reincarnation?

FRANK: No. I believe that every human being is unrepeatable.

JAY: Like a dirty story. Well, actually the existence of ghosts has been recently proved. (A little groggy due to FRANK's resemblance to Ed) Very recently.

FRANK: No kidding. (Gets up, examining apartment) Hey, whaddaya pay here?

JAY: Ya pays your dues. (Apologizing for mess) I used to keep plants. Man-eating plants. They starved. (HE gets FRANK's coffee accidentally, makes a face, grabs his own)

FRANK: (Who is getting none of JAY's jokes) No kidding. Hey, what are these, mystic books?

JAY: What are what?

FRANK: These with the Egyptian titles.

JAY: (Baffled) Egyptian which?

FRANK: Aak-Abu, Aca-Bek, Bel-Cav . . .

JAY: (Joins FRANK at bookcase) THOSE are an encyclopedia. What are you, anyway, hipped on the occult?

FRANK: (Embarrassed) Uh, no—but John said that you were interested in ghosts and spirits and like that, and that I should discuss it with you.

JAY: Isn't that typical of Jo Wanda? You want to do in a generous friend; you send them a poisoned opportunist.

FRANK: But who was it you were talking to? That guy that died?

JAY: (Visibly shaken) Jo Wanda does tell all, doesn't she? No, it was somebody trying to sell me something on the phone. (Indicates script in FRANK's back pocket) What have you got there, her dossier on me?

FRANK: (Shyly, handing it to JAY) No . . . that's MY play.

JAY: Plays. I love them. (Flings it backwards over his shoulder, is about to say something really scathing to FRANK. Phone rings. Answers it as before) What's the matter, Jo Wanda, didn't you have time to teach him the Southern accent? (Hangs up, wraps phone in its own cord, jams it in wastebasket, turns back to the puzzled but charmed FRANK) So, you write too?

FRANK: Well, not really, not yet. That's what I came here for.

JAY: Here? Tonight?

FRANK: Ha. No, I mean here to New York.

JAY: (Quickly, to Ghost, to FRANK's bewilderment) Listen, baby, they're playing our song. (To FRANK) And how do you LIKE New York?

FRANK: (Whenever attention is focussed on him, HE automatically becomes charming) Oh, well, all I've seen of it so far, really, is between John's house and here—

JAY: Gay Street.

FRANK: Right. Gee, it sure is busy for such a cold night. All those people walking up and down the street. Such a dark little street, too—(His naivete on the subject is slightly assumed)

JAY: Yeah, well, it's one of those nights.

FRANK: One of what nights?

JAY: Monday, Tuesday, Wednesday, Thursday, Friday—

FRANK: (Quickly) Ha! (Philosophical) What are they all looking for?

JAY: (After deadly pause) Approval?

FRANK: Ha! (Changing subject) John SAID you were a pretty good writer. (Heads for Ed's papers) Is that your stuff on the desk?

JAY: (Hopping between FRANK and desk) No, that's the literary leavings of that "dead guy" you mentioned.

FRANK: Oh. John said he was pretty good, too.

JAY: (High-queen) Well, I don't think Jo Wanda could have meant his writing.

      FRANK makes a piqued face.

You don't like my calling John "Jo Wanda"?

FRANK: Frankly, no.

JAY: Daring of you to fly in the face of convention that way. Okay (Mock butch) Woddidja call 'im at college?

FRANK: Mr. Lawrence.

JAY: Oh, Mary!

FRANK: Well, he was a senior when I was a freshman.

JAY: Wasn't everybody? I mean, you're awfully young, aren't you? As it were?

FRANK: Well, I'm almost twenty.

JAY: (Beginning a snide inquisition) And out of college? My!

FRANK: Well, no—I—left school when I was a sophomore.

JAY: Oh? And ever since?

FRANK: Well, gee, that's only been six months. I wasn't much of a
　　　student, I guess. (Laughs, JAY joins in. Serious) I wanted to see
　　　more of life than I was at school. Hell, YOU know—

JAY: (Understandingly) Mmm.

FRANK: So I—knocked around on the coast for a few months—

JAY: The West Coast.

FRANK: Yeah, San Francisco.

JAY: Ah. And—?

FRANK: (Feeling uninteresting, for once) Well, that's all. Gee, I don't
　　　want to talk about myself. What do YOU do? Besides write, I
　　　mean? Say, I'd sure like to see your stuff.

JAY: Oh, I'm still knocking around on this coast—quietly. We don't
　　　want to start reading to each other—(Picks up boy's play and
　　　places it under Ed's huge pile of papers)—DO we?

FRANK: I would like you to have a look at my play. John thought
　　　maybe you could help me to—

JAY: (Grabbing cup of coffee, cigarettes, anything) My hands are full
right now.

　　　　　This is enough of an insult for even FRANK to see. THEY
　　　　　stand embarrassedly facing one another for a minute.

FRANK: Oh.

BOTH (Simultaneously) Well—(THEY laugh, but the tension is not
　　　broken. Brief pause and THEY speak together again)

FRANK: (Referring to the Kandinsky) Who did that?

JAY (Simultaneous) What time do you have? (THEY laugh)

FRANK: Nine to five.

JAY: (Simultaneous) Kandinsky. (THEY laugh) Nine to five. Great odds. (To FRANK, with Bette Davis imitation, exactly as at start of play) Do you like it?

FRANK: (Studying picture intently) Well, I don't know; I never understand that stuff. (Charmingly) Maybe you could explain it to me?

> JAY trembles, turns away. This has all happened before.

> Or did you have somewhere to go? Hey, am I putting you out?

JAY: No, I wasn't turned on. No no no, not at all. (With sincere warmth and graciousness, an elaborate Oriental bow) You're welcome.

FRANK: (Warmly) Thank you.

JAY: (Repeats gesture sketchily) You're welcome. No, I never go out anymore, everything comes to ME. (Trying to close everything off without rancour) Look, you're probably anxious to get some sleep—

GUEST: OH, gee, no, not my first night here. I thought I'd go out—if I only knew where to go!

JAY: (Remembering his original mission, to get rid of boy) Uh—you know, New York is really a terribly dull town—you can ask Jo— John! It's terribly overrated.

FRANK: (Acres of charm) Aw, I bet it's not, not if you have the right kind of person to show you around.

JAY: (Coldly) Look, if you really want to "see more of life," as you said, you should get yourself a travelling job. Like with the World Health Organization? W.H.O.? WHO needs you.

FRANK: (Obviously hurt) Oh—

JAY: (Embarrassed) Look, I'm being—overly rude. Do you want the bathroom or anything? The little boys' room is right through here—and mine is just beyond.

FRANK: No, not right now, thanks.

JAY: (Trying to make him feel at ease) Have you eaten?

FRANK: Yeah, yeah, I did already, thanks.

JAY: Well, would you like to write something? I must have a pencil around here someplace—(Mock scrabble through a drawer)

FRANK: (Chuckles) Ha! No, thanks.

JAY: (A little desperate) Well, I haven't any music—

FRANK: (Brightly) I could tell you about my bus trip from Iowa!

JAY: (Instantly, self-preservation) Would you like some drugs?

FRANK: Uh, gee—I don't know—what?

JAY: (Mock offense) My dear, I was joking! (Whips open well-stocked drug cabinet) Would you?

FRANK: (Terrified, trying to appear sophisticated) Uh—well—I don't know. What is it, Mary Jane?

JAY: (Scathingly) Yes, "Mary Jane." This particular kind is called "boo." (As one connoisseur to another) Do you know it?

FRANK: Uh, well—yeah—sure—I had it—a couple of times—once.

JAY: Ah! And how did you find it? Cool?

FRANK: Well, to tell you the truth, it made me—drowsy.

JAY: Oh, that's easy—(Whips out pills) Have one of these!

FRANK: What are they?

JAY: (Offers some) They're heaven. Try it. It's a mild stimulant—compared to some. (Mock scientific) Counteracts the drowsiness.

FRANK: (Reluctantly takes a couple in his palm) How can you take this stuff?

JAY: (Flips FRANK's palm up so the pills go down FRANK's throat) Like this! (As FRANK sputters and gulps coffee) Oh, come on, anything I can take, you can take!

FRANK: It's an up?

JAY: It's an out!

FRANK: It'll keep me awake?

JAY: Only for the first seventy-two hours. (FRANK is terrified) I'm joking. No, you can sleep if you want to, after the first couple of hours. Give it, say, thirty minutes to hit. Here, we can make your bed while we wait. Up!

> THEY fold down the sofa and make it up as a bed, or rather FRANK does, as JAY neatly stands by and dances with snapping fingers.

FRANK: Did you ever—

JAY: (Throws pillow at him) Wanna pillow?

FRANK: Did you ever—

JAY: (Throws another pillow) Wanna fight?

FRANK: Did you ever try—

JAY: Wanna pillow fight?

FRANK: Did you ever try acid?

JAY: Yes—once. You don't want to try that. (Enacts this story vividly as FRANK makes bed) It was fine at first. The walls turned all fluorescent paisley mauve, and then the ceiling opened and a flight of golden stairs descended, and angels with silver trumpets heralded the arrival of the Great God Jehovah—and here He came! All white, flowing beard, His arms held out to ME!

FRANK: (Beginning to get off, awed) Wow!

JAY: (High-queen) And there I was—on acid! (HE hops down from the back of the sofa, where HE has ended up, and dances giddily about the room)

FRANK: Uh, this stuff won't make me dizzy, will it?

JAY: No, I'm like this all the time. I'm joking No, it DOES have a couple of side effects. It tends to make one talk rather loosely and honestly—and of course, if anybody hits a tuning-fork, you disappear, and—oh! The first half hour or so after it hits, it tends —in certain isolated cases—to bring out the sex urge in one—(Dives onto the bed, mock Yvonne De Carlo)—or more.

FRANK: Uh, look—there's something I really ought to tell you.

JAY: What? (Having fun making FRANK uncomfortable)

FRANK: If you don't mind my asking—

JAY: (Super-sultry) Honey, I never mind anybody asking.

FRANK: It's—

JAY: Yeeeeees?

FRANK: (Frankly) Are you a homosexual?

JAY: (Casually) Don't mention it.

FRANK: No, are you?

JAY: (Grabbing an ostrich fan or fur piece from somewhere) Do I LOOK like a homosexual?

FRANK: Please don't be offended—there's just so much of it around.

JAY: (Dispensing with prop) Well, it ain't contagious—relax.

FRANK: Please, let me tell you how I feel—

JAY: Honey, I don't want to feel you.

FRANK: You see, when I was in college I took psychiatry—

JAY: —and vice versa—

FRANK: Why are you so defensive?

JAY: Because you're so offensive!

FRANK: No, you're just taking offense.

JAY: Well, I'm not taking any more! Now relax, Mr. District Attorney, whatever you may think you've got on me, I have twice as much on you.

FRANK: Anything you think you have on me is strictly in your imagination!

JAY: Don't be ridiculous, in my imagination I have nothing on you. Now, wait, I'm only joking. You shouldn't assume that every homosexual wants to sleep with every attractive boy he meets— just because a few million of us are like that.

FRANK: Tell me, did you ever see a psychiatrist?

JAY: You mean one of those people who tell you society is sick and then offer to help you adjust to it?

FRANK: You don't have to be crazy to see a psychiatrist. I'd like to see one myself.

JAY: (Holds out hand) You're pseudoagressive — that'll be five thousand dollars.

FRANK: What you have is a persecution complex.

JAY: What I have is a complex persecution.

FRANK: But did you ever think of seeing a psychiatrist?

JAY: (As if hallucinating) I think I see a psychiatrist!

FRANK: For instance, do you know what psychiatrists say about people who wear unattractive clothes?

JAY: (Stung) Do YOU know what they say about people who don't wear underwear?

FRANK: I wear underwear! Oh, you're just being hostile!

JAY: Yeah, youth hostel!

FRANG: I think people and homosexuals should try to understand one another!

JAY: Ho, boy! People on this side, homosexuals over here!

FRANK: I think the homosexual—

JAY: THE homosexual? Who he?

FRANK: I think the homosexual should find his place in society!

JAY: Where? Off-Broadway?

FRANK: I should think the homosexual—

JAY: THE?

FRANK: —would be tired of being persecuted!

JAY: You noticed!

FRANK: You're evading my question!

JAY: No, I'm ignoring it!

FRANK: ARE you a homosexual?

JAY: I'm THE homosexual!

FRANK: Now, look—

JAY: You look! There's a question I've always wanted to ask someone.

FRANK: What is it?

JAY: I hope you won't be offended.

FRANK: Well, what? No, of course not, What?

JAY: Well—you're heterosexual, aren't you?

FRANK: Sure!

JAY: Now, don't get angry, I'm only satisfying my curiosity—or perhaps I should say I'm satisfying only my curiosity—

FRANK: Oh, come on—

JAY: Tell me, Frank, how long have you BEEN heterosexual?

FRANK: What do you mean? I've ALWAYS been heterosexual!

JAY: Started as a kid, huh? Tsk-tsk. Tell me, do you think one of your teachers, or possibly even one of your parents might have been heterosexual? Do you think that might have been the reason you—

FRANK: (Interrupting) All right, all right, just shut up, okay?

JAY: Okay, Frank. Gee, I didn't think you'd be so touchy about it. Wow. (Brief pause) Tell me, is your play heterosexual?

FRANK: (Snappy) You mean does it sleep with plays of the opposite sex?

JAY: (Delighted to have drawn wit) Oooo. Getting off, ain'tcha? Well, you know, you people DO tend to let heterosexuality CREEP into all your work.

FRANK: What are you talking about? You people are flagrant!

JAY: Homosexuals are flagrant? Did you ever see a Puerto Rican wedding?

FRANK: I think you ought to see a psychiatrist—fast!

JAY: Why are you so anxious to see me on a couch?

FRANK: Because you're a nice person and I'd like to see you happy.

JAY: (Does hideous grin) There! Now you see it. (Frowns) And now you don't! (Before FRANK can reply) Look, will you fold up that obscene couch? Like the Playmate of the Month, dear. I've got to go and get some cigarette papers to wrap this baby bunting in. (Starts off—stops) But first, there IS one more question I'd like to ask you—

FRANK: Jesus, what?

JAY: College, Coast, cross-country—haven't you HAD your homosexual experience?

FRANK: That's my business!

JAY: Funny. I would have sworn you were an amateur. (HE exits with grass)

FRANK: Look, I am trying to preserve my dignity—

JAY: (Sticks his head back in) Yeah? What was it like? (Quick exit)

> FRANK, alone, angrily finishes folding up couch. Then HE stalks over to Ed's papers, extracts his play. In doing so, HE has to lift Ed's bundle. HE weighs Ed's enormous output against his own slim script, puts both down. Slowly HE allows himself to look into a mirror cross-stage. HE goes over, combs his hair thoroughly, tries unbuttoning a button or two, nods with approval at the effect, then saunters back to the desk. HE extracts one of Ed's poems, reads it, sneers. Reads another, says, "Oh, come on." Reads another, mocks its apparently mechanical meter: "De-dum, de-dum, de-dum". HE is feeling pretty self-satisfied right now. HE draws out another poem, starts to sneer—but it is apparently good.

FRANK: (Yells) Hey! This guy's no good, huh?

JAY: (Pops in) You have taste. He was a great reefer-roller, though.

> FRANK quickly hides the poem behind him and follows JAY around the room.

I am out of cigarette papers. I would rather be out of toilet paper.

FRANK: But you kept all that stuff of his, huh?

JAY: It was here. Now, where is that hookah?

> JAY is searching for hookah. FRANK follows him, being
> terribly "nice" and "interested."

FRANK: Oh, were you and him—?

JAY: I never touched him! (Menacingly) And THAT man is dead.
(Returns to search) Hookah, hookah, hookah.

FRANK: Well, what was he—good-looking?

JAY: He was as handsome as the NEXT man. Ah, here it is! (HE takes
lampshade off huge hookah. Explaining) I get so paranoid
sometimes!

> JAY sits down to arrange hookah. FRANK extends his script.

FRANK: I'd like you to look at my play.

> JAY takes it, literally "looks at it," front and back, lays it on
> floor and sets hookah on top of it.

FRANK: (Laughs good-naturedly) Ha! Uh—how'd you meet him?

JAY: (Preparing hookah) It was a very unique meeting. He was an old
frat friend of Jo Wanda's—a very, very, VERY (HE sucks at
hookah to make his point) good friend of Jo Wanda's—so BURT
sent him over to spend the night with me.

FRANK: Oh, I see . . . How'd he die?

JAY: (Shocked) Alone.

FRANK: Oh. Suicide?

JAY: (This is really too much for him) No, thanks, I just had one.
People on this side, homosexuals over here. Wanna play Red Rover?

FRANK: You know, you're really very funny.

JAY: (Thrusting hookah mouthpiece at him) I take drugs.

FRANK: Uh, no thanks. You better start it. I like to watch.

JAY: Thanks, baby.

> HE does the ritual of lighting hookah, making sure it draws,
> etc. FRANK watches, fascinated. JAY is struck by the
> similarity of this to scenes with Ed, repeats, "Thanks, baby,"
> then after a drag, in Southern accent, affectionately:

Ah wish you wouldn't call me "baby."

FRANK: (Puzzled) I didn't call you—

JAY: (Quickly) I know, I know; I, Jo Wanda did. I'm glad it cost her a
unit, the eunuch!

FRANK: I thought John was your friend.

JAY: So she is (Takes drag)

FRANK: Then why do you knock him?

JAY: Because she's so flat—and wooden—and closed.

FRANK: That's awful!

JAY: No, it's just her way. Here, smoke.

FRANK: Uh—maybe I had better just watch.

JAY (Jams stem in FRANK's mouth) No, join me—because I am coming
apart. Boy, those pills hit like bowling balls!

> FRANK coughs on smoke. JAY grins. FRANK tries again,
> determined to do it. HE continues to smoke throughout the
> next sequence.

JAY: Here, you need one of these (Gives FRANK 'popper' inhaler)

FRANK: What is it?

JAY: Oh, just a little something to filter the New York air.

FRANK: Is this stuff dangerous?

JAY: No more than mother's milk—if you know your Freud.

FRANK: Yeah, I'm getting a terrific—uh (Snaps his fingers, trying to think of word, is delighted when he does) rush!

JAY: Not from me, toots.

FRANK: Hey, is it getting hot in here, or is it just me?

JAY: I don't know—let's open yon window and see.

FRANK: What's life like in Greenwich Village?

JAY: Nothing's very lifelike in Greenwich Village. (HE giggles, goes to window, takes a hammer, pulls out nails, which have kept window closed, and flings it open. JAY looks down on the crowded street below. FRANK continues to smoke.)

Ah, there they are. My people, my puppets, my pageant, my parade! Hello, everyone. I love you all, every one of you, little six pointed creatures like snowflakes, each slightly different—even if you are all alike. Up and down, down and down, round and round, over and out! (HE observes, and calls FRANK's attention to a pick-up between a "fem" and a "butch") Oooh, lookie! Mince-mince-mince. Lumber-lumber-lumber. Mince—mince. Lumber—lumber. ("Fem" slows down) Miiiiince. ("Butch" slows down) Luuuuumber. ("Fem" approaches "Butch") Mince-mince-mince. ("Butch" approaches "Fem") Lumber-lumber-lumber. ("Butch" and "Fem" walk off together) Mince-lumber, mince-lumber, mince-lumber! (HE claps his hands in joy)

FRANK: (Looking out of the window) Can't we go out?

JAY: Not that way!

FRANK: All my life I wanted to get to New York.

JAY: And what was your second wish?

103

FRANK: To meet interesting people.

JAY: (Indicating street) Drop a handkerchief.

FRANK: (Trying to make up, softly stoned) Look, you don't think I hold it against you, your being homosexual.

JAY: Well, you can't be homosexual in a vacuum.

FRANK: You can't help being homosexual.

JAY: (Retreating a bit from this puzzling intimacy) Sometimes I can.

FRANK: I can't help being heterosexual.

JAY: Is that final?

FRANK: I didn't come over here to judge you—

JAY: You'll notice I didn't get into my bathing suit.

FRANK: I'd like us to be friends.

JAY: Three wishes and out.

FRANK: Please don't be flip. (HE is in a pot-benevolent mood)

JAY: Well, all right, Frank. Look, now that we're being buddies—

FRANK: Are you going to start again—?

JAY: There's one question I've really always wanted to ask—

FRANK: You're going to start needling me again—

JAY: What do straight boys DO together?

FRANK: You're needling me.

JAY: (Mock pique) Golly, how can I be a writer when I grow up if no one will answer my questions?

FRANK: Oh, well, I guess—if I was with a friend—buddy—pal—on a Saturday night, we'd go—I don't know—bowling—beer-drinking—looking for girls—

JAY: I guess everybody I know is still looking for the friend.

FRANK: Or—(Has begun to fan himself with Ed's poem)

JAY: Yeah?

FRANK: If it was a really good friend—(HE is turning on the charm)

JAY: Yeah? Yeah?

FRANK: One that I liked and trusted—

JAY: Mm-hm.

FRANK: —and who shared my interests—

JAY: Go on—

FRANK: And if the mood was right—

    JAY nods, fascinated.

We'd probably read our manuscripts to each other!

JAY: You can quit fanning yourself, Scarlett, you just blew it. (Of Ed's poem) Hey, what is that?

FRANK: Oh, I have to admit—I sort of liked this one.

JAY: (Snatching it from him) Come on, nobody's THAT young. (Glances at poem) Oh, well, no wonder. This is a note of mine. I have the whole poem here somewhere! (HE goes to a drawer in the desk and starts taking out huge, neat piles—his own manuscripts)

FRANK: (Wandering over, fascinated) Wow, you must have liked that guy a lot!

JAY: (Seeking a certain manuscript) Maybe I killed him to get his priceless manuscripts.

FRANK: Not with all those! . . . He killed himself, didn't he?

JAY: ("Are we back on that?") I went down to the 9th Precinct to inquire on that very point. And for the next eleven hours I was group therapy for a gang of cops. (Still searching)

FRANK: That must have been rough.

JAY: They'd like you to think so.

FRANK: I mean with your friend dead and all . . . Why did they question YOU?

JAY: (Still searching) They thunk I done it.

FRANK: Ha! . . . You didn't, did you?

JAY: (Not believing what he is hearing) Didn't WHAT?

FRANK: Kill him?

JAY: Not yet! (Finds poem) Ah! Now, stick that thing in your mouth and listen! (HE hands hookah to FRANK, quickly drops FRANK's play into wastebasket without FRANK noticing, grabs a chair to stand on, and reads with considerable dramatic power and bravura)

THE READERS OF CAHIERS DU CINEMA
ALL LINED UP TO GET THEIR ENEMA!

FRANK: That's great! Great!

JAY: That's the title.

FRANK: Great title!

JAY: (Reads on)
Jimmy lived for films of terror,
After homework without error.

This Phi Beta Kappa member went
Mad for visions of dismemberment.
Disembodied living brains,
Dangling ganglia like chains,
Flew on naked girls to twist 'em
In their naked nervous system.
Virgin Jim watched showgirls' shadows
Being torn apart in grottoes
By robots who, though they adored 'em,
Had no other uses for 'em.
Citizenshipped, summa-cum-lauded,
Jimmy only was rewarded
Watching boys robbed of their features
To endow unviable creatures!
Jimmy's parents read an article,
And accepted every particle.
They believed, with the majority,
Monsters really killed Authority.
At the horror show they found him,
Happy children all around him,
Extracted him, and set two strictures:
He must not WANT to see such pictures!
They locked Jim in with his studies,
Thinking him and all his buddies
Willful, free, seditious errants,
Learning to destroy their parents.
They mis-studied freak creation,
And misread externalization;
Sublimation is its thesis:
Jimmy tore HIMSELF to pieces!

> JAY has acted out every line, leapt about on furniture,
> become monsters, Jimmy, showgirls, and parents. As a finale,
> HE tears the poem to shreds and fling it in the air.

FRANK: Great! Just great! Great! (Applauds, stamps his feet, subsides)
I can't write poetry.

JAY: How did we get back to YOU?

FRANK: But John says I'm pretty good.

JAY: Hmmm. Well, your profile's not bad, you could pose for coins.

FRANK: I mean writing.

HAY: Just as long as you don't mean reading.

FRANK: You mean you don't want to hear my play?

JAY: E.S.P.!

FRANK' (Hurt) Hey!

JAY: E.S.P., baby: Everybody Smoke Pot!

FRANK: Buy my play! (Looks about for it)

JAY: (Memory) Play! (Starts digging through manuscripts again)

FRANK: Everybody at school thought I was a good writer. My English teacher used to have me over to his house nights!

JAY: (High-queen) Yeah, I heard about him from Jo Wanda!

FRANK: I am a good writer, goddamit! I'm the best fuckin' writer around!

JAY: How's your writing?

FRANK: You're queer!

JAY: You're high!

FRANK: I'm not!

JAY: I am.

FRANK: You are?

JAY: We are. Sit down! (Shoves him onto sofa)

FRANK: Hey, what the hell did you do to my play?

JAY: (Finds what he is looking for) Play! (Comes up with three huge bound manuscripts)

FRANK: Don't you really want to hear it? (HE is looking everywhere)

JAY: Sure, baby, and you can hear it, too! What a Beautiful Planet, the People Who Live Here Must Be Very Happy. A Trilogy by Jay Astor!

> FRANK sees the enormous manuscript and redoubles his efforts to find his own. JAY reads on, changing his voice for each character, reading rapid-fire.

"The setting is a dingy hotel room. A blonde lolls on the bed. A man enters, slams and locks the door. HE: I don't believe this neighbourhood is safe; everyone I passed was in plain clothes. SHE: Our problem, Jake, is I want to commit adultery and you just want to dishonor your father and mother! HE: Oh, shut up, Elvira; I haven't had so much fun since incest became a motif!"

FRANK: (Finds his manuscript in the wastebasket. In disbelief) Who ARE you?

JAY: (Triumphantly) "SHE:"

SCENE 2

> Lights up almost immediately. JAY is still reading, from the last page of the last volume. FRANK lies on the couch, stoned, smoking, covered with sheets of manuscripts.

JAY: "HE: Half the fun of sex is getting your clothes off. SHE: And most of the other half is having them off. HE: I'll hate myself in the morning. SHE: It is morning. HE: And—I hate myself. Curtain." Applause. Acclaim, Irreparable immortality.

FRANK: (Weakly, sincerely) Great. Great. Great. The greatest.

JAY: (Picking up the litter) I presume you mean the greater.

FRANK: Great, really great. You are amazing.

JAY: Yeah, well, don't drool on my poems. (Picking them off FRANK)

FRANK: THEY'RE great! Everything you showed me is great.

JAY: Everything you showed me is great too!

FRANK: Why haven't you DONE anything?

JAY: (Mock pass) Why, honey, I thought you didn't want me to.

FRANK: I mean—

JAY: I know, I know— (Continues picking up)

FRANK: You keep saying, "I know, I know."

JAY: Well, if there's one thing I do, it's know.

FRANK: Whadda you know?

JAY: I know I'm seven years older than you.

FRANK: So?

JAY: So, haven't you learned anything since you were thirteen?

FRANK: Yeah. Jesus, you always win, don't you?

JAY: Sure, you play fair.

FRANK: No kidding, I mean it. You're great. You're a great actor, too.
I feel like I really saw your play. Did you ever want to act?

JAY: No. It just happens, they did offer me the comic lead in Oh!
Calcutta. But I didn't want him.

FRANK: That lead part is fantastic. Burt would be right for it.

JAY: Honey, Burt would be right INSTEAD of it.

FRANK: Really, you have a future.

JAY: I've had enough of my future, thank you.

FRANK: Seriously, what are you wasting yourself for?

JAY: (To put an end to this) Well, I came to New York to write and sing and dance and act and paint.

FRANK: And what happened?

JAY: I'm available for any parts for writing, singing, dancing, acting painters. Any new business?

FRANK: Can't you be serious?

JAY: I had it removed.

FRANK: You don't even seem to take my compliments seriously.

JAY: (Mock pass) Well, they're all talk.

FRANK: Christ, if I had all your talents—

JAY: Judas, you've had most of them—

FRANK: I can't write nearly as well as you—

JAY: You keep saying that like it was a virtue.

FRANK: All I've got is this one play! (Holds it up like a torch)

JAY: (Makes FRANK take the play in his arms and hold it to his breast) Then you must hold it and keep it and cherish and nurture it, and never show it to anyone—(Shoves him away)—or else!

FRANK: (Beyond insult) You're great at this flip talk, too—you know, I'm really glad John sent me over here—(HE has followed JAY into a corner and now takes JAY's shoulders affectionately) No one has asked me to stay overnight for years.

JAY: (Human, after all, in the arms of a stoned, admiring youth) Stay overnight for years. (Mock-faints and crawls away)

FRANK: (All concern) Gee, what happened?

JAY: (Defending himself with a wooden chair, like a lion tamer) I recoil from affection.

FRANK: Are you all right?

JAY: (Mimicking FRANK's inflection) I'm great! (Cornered again, FRANK advancing admiringly) Uh, look—what's that play of yours about?

FRANK: (Crosses to get it from where it dropped when HE rushed to help JAY) Oh, it's about this guy and this girl—and she's very conventional and narrowminded—and he pulls out—

JAY: (To no one) Anticlimactic.

FRANK: It's based on actual experience . . . Do you really want to hear it?

JAY: Need you ask?

FRANK: Well, gosh—gee—wow—okay—here goes—(HE unconsciously imitates JAY's reading posture) It doesn't have a title—

JAY: Mmm. I like that.

FRANK: Oh, really? Well, maybe. Here goes—"Act One, Scene One. SHE: Hello—"

JAY: No, I don't like that.

FRANK: Huh? What?

JAY: "Hello." No. Sorry.

FRANK: But it's just—it's just—it's just—

JAY: I don't care if it's just or not; I don't like it. Haven't you got any stage directions?

FRANK: Sure, later on—

JAY: No no no. Get into it right off. It should be something like—"Act One, Scene One. SHE: Parenthesis. Enters, tender as the morning star, her hair sprinkled with rain, in a tone which instantly tells us that she has left her duck-tailed boyfriend waiting out in a light spring rain in his two-tone 1963 Mercury coupe, so that she can come in and beg her stern, grey-haired stockbroker father to let

112

her PLEASE go to the opening of the new Pizza Parlor because it is, after all, her birthday and she hasn't had any fun since Mama ran away to join the roller derby. Close parenthesis. 'Hello.' " (Pause) No, it's the "Hello" that's wrong.

FRANK: How can "Hello" be wrong?

JAY: You'd be surprised. Let's see; it should be something dynamic, bracing, youthful, intoxicating, alive, all the things I know you want this girl to be. "Hi?" "How's tricks?" "This is a stickup." No, no, no! Let me think. Girl, girl, girl. What, what, what? Maybe, maybe, maybe. No, no, no. Wait! I've got it. (Becomes "Girl") "Hello, hello, hello!" No, it just doesn't say "girl" to me! (Sits in mock concentration)

FRANK: (Bitterly) Do you KNOW any girls?

JAY: The moment I see one.

FRANK: I guess you don't like girls?

JAY: Well, I wouldn't want my sister to marry one.

FRANK: (Trying to regain his composure) I mean, I guess you see them as rivals for—

JAY: Yes, go on, for whom?

FRANK: I have trouble expressing myself—

JAY: Is that your only recommendation as a writer?

FRANK: I have trouble talking to people—

JAY: Why don't you try telling the truth?

FRANK: Well, look, if you do know some girls, maybe you could introduce me to—

JAY: I beg your pardon! Haven't I introduced you to enough tonight?

FRANK: Christ! I don't know why you people are that way! I should think you'd want to help younger people.

113

JAY: Yeah, younger and younger!

FRANK: (Extends play) Why won't you—?

JAY: (Grabs anything) I told you, mac, my hands are full!

FRANK: Of what? What have you got to do?

JAY: I've got a lot of nerves to break down—and you're not helping! What are you doing here, anyway? Who told you that you could write?

FRANK: Well, who told YOU?

JAY: YOU did!

FRANK: You wanna know what I think?

JAY: I wanna know WHETHER you think!

FRANK: I think the reason you're being like this is because you want somethin' from me that you know you're not gonna get!

JAY: What have YOU been smoking?

FRANK: Come on; I got all those cracks you've been making, and I know about John, and Burt, and you.

JAY: Sugarplum, I want your tender white body about as much as I want anything in this world! And I presume by now you know how much THAT is.

FRANK: Oh, yeah? Then how come you're takin' all this time with me?

JAY: I like to look at you.

FRANK: How come you read me all your stuff?

JAY: I like to listen to MYSELF!

FRANK: Christ, trying to get you people to be serious is murder!

JAY: Or be killed.

FRANK: How can a guy get anything done? All I want is to write about the world as I see it!

JAY: The world will sue.

FRANK: To write honestly! Truthfully! Fearlessly! (On each word HE bangs the rolled up script in the palm of his hand)

JAY: I'LL sue!

FRANK: (Pacing) And you ask someone to give you just a little help. . . and they're all either tied up with their home life, like Jo Wanda, or else they're too beat and scared and shy like you. Christ! I just want to write. Honestly! (Whack) Truthfully! (Whack) Fearlessly (Whack) And all I get is a lot of hurt sensitivities and wisecracks! And people waste their lives sitting around talking to themselves about how wasted their lives are, and you ask 'em to help you not waste yours and they tell you their hands are full! Christ! The world is dying for someone who writes honestly! (Whack) And truthfully! (Whack) And—

> JAY echoes the words and mimics the actions on the last "Honestly, Truthfully" bit, which so enrages FRANK that HE flings the script at JAY, striking rather hard.

JAY: Oho!

> HE hops up as if to do battle. FRANK, appalled at his own rashness, stands terrified. JAY lets him quiver for an instant, then snaps into "high-queen".

Is my semi-precious stoned?

> FRANK gives a moan and falls down on the sofa, buries his face, frustrated, enraged. JAY picks up FRANK's script and is about to throw it out the window but relents, satisfies himself with hiding it behind a shutter, stands looking at the nearly-weeping boy.

(To Ghost) I'm sorry. (To FRANK, who slowly rises in anger, thinking the epithets are directed at him) What a rotten, miserable, lying, self-pitying son of a bitch—(Smiles)— I am. (Goes to FRANK) Hey, let's leave this place to the graveyard shift, huh? Wouldja like to see the village?

FRANK: (Pouty) I thought you never went out.

JAY: Honey, I talk so much it can't all be true. Don't you want to see the Village? I mean, it's just downstairs. We can even bring some of it up.

FRANK: Yeah. I'd like to see the Village. I guess that sounds corny to you.

JAY: Alice, you say one more sincere thing and I'll throw you out of Wonderland and stop up my hole! Come on, get that awful coat; I'll get us in backstage at Burt's theatre.

FRANK: (Excited) Can you?

JAY: Sure, would you like that?

FRANK: Yeah, really, because I want to write, honestly I do. And so I want to see all the shows and meet all the people and get to writing right off, because I don't want to wind up like you and Jo Wanda, just sitting around moping . . . I'm sorry.

JAY: Forget it: I don't want to be like you, either. Get your things.

FRANK: Hey, I didn't mean that. I just meant you've gone to pot!

> They laugh. FRANK is again embracing JAY, who is again leery of it.

JAY: I said this stuff makes you honest.

FRANK: I'm sorry. Because I like you, I really do—

JAY: Yeah, well, those things are said. Come on, let's go before I do. something I'll regret the rest of the night! Go get that horrible coat!

> FRANK just stands laughing, loving every word JAY says.

Come on, come on, the pot thickens!

FRANK: (Stumbling off beaming) You are great!

JAY: (Alone, goes to door, presses buzzer and shouts into mouthpiece) Help!

FRANK: Re-enters with coat, stumbling) Wow, I shouldn't have moved, I'm dizzy. How long will this last?

JAY: (Mutters) Another ten years unless I do something quick!

FRANK: What?

JAY: ("Let us be gay!") What? What? What? Don't try to catch every little word. Just watch the movement they make, round and round and round to confuse you, but really down into the depths! (Swirls FRANK in a low tango dip)

FRANK: Can you really get me into the theatre?

JAY: Stick with me, kid, and I'll have your name up in lights—even if I have to change it to Annette Funicello. (Or appropriate look-alike movie actress for boy)

FRANK: (Runs to mirror, laughing) Annette Funicello? Annette Funicello?

JAY: (Laughs, grabs his hand, leads him running around room) Come on, Alice, come on! You can't get to Wonderland through the Looking-Glass! Come on, Alice, we're late! Round and round and round and down the rabbit hole!

> THEY spin in a little dance and then fall in a pile on the floor, FRANK on top of JAY, giggling like a fool. JAY suddenly stops laughing, shoves him away, stands, runs to opposite side of room.

My God. My dear God.

FRANK: Huh?

JAY: I wasn't talking to you.

FRANK: (Staggers to his feet, dragging his coat) Come on, let's go out.

JAY: Yeah, you with a whimper and me without a bang.

FRANK: Huh? Aren't we going out?

JAY: That's what they say—and I know why!

FRANK: Why, what?

JAY: Who? Which? When? Where? I did it.

FRANK: Did what?

JAY: You didn't do it; I did it. I did it again just now.

FRANK: What?

JAY: Weren't you going somewhere?

FRANK: Where?

JAY: I don't know, where?

FRANK: Hey, what's wrong?

JAY: Technically, nothing. It's a superb reproduction.

FRANK: Of what? (FRANK is dizzy with confusion now)

JAY: Do I have to let you kill me this time? That'll only mean your
     turn comes up again next time!

> FRANK looks blankly at JAY, then fumbles over to the sofa
> and passes out. JAY shamefacedly picks up FRANK's jacket
> and is about to cover the sleeping boy with it, when suddenly
> HE begins talking aloud, sometimes to the Ghost, sometimes
> to the sleeping FRANK, sometimes to the jacket, sometimes
> to himself.

The amazing thing is that anyone as smart as I supposedly am
could have been stupid enough all this time to lay the blame on
YOU! You, teasing and tantalizing me out of my peace of mind,
without even offering a piece of—well, let that pass! (To FRANK)
I don't want your body, I've got one of my own! (Glances in
mirror) Well, let that pass, too! (To Ghost, about FRANK,
lecherously) I've got half a mind to—(To FRANK) But then you've
got half a mind, too. (To jacket) You've got this body and I've got
this mind and love will make us one. (To Ghost) One what? Very

funny! (To FRANK) But what if it should have my body and your mind? Oh, shut up. (To himself) My trouble is I'm of two minds—(To jacket) With but a single thought. (Screams, throwing jacket across room) BUTT OUT! Butt out! I am trying to coordinate! (To FRANK) How dare you come in here and pull me apart just when I'm about to pull myself together? (To Ghost) I could be very happy together! (HE is by now talking to the air, focusing nowhere in particular) People can be happy together, you know! Yes they can! Yes they can! Didn't you ever see the Late Late Show? Of course it depends on which one you catch. You watch the wrong movies and wow! (Becomes Bette Davis) I won't let you go. (Paul Henreid) Try to be an adult, Madeleine; there's nothing you can do to stop me. (Bette Davis) There is — one thing I can do. (Henreid) Madeleine—put down that tiny, pearl-handled revolver. (Davis) If I can't have you, nobody can!

> HE has been hopping from position to position to play this scene. Now HE shoots as Bette, then hops over to fall as Paul. "She" shoots "him" several times, bringing him lower each time—until JAY is hopping from side to side of the room, shooting and screaming. HE finally screams as himself and gets under control.

(To GHOST) Well, people can be happy. We were, weren't we? Gadding about the Village to keep away from un-neutral territory —"Your place or mine?"—or finally, when we'd seen every movie south of Fourteenth Street and none of them, not one of them, had helped, sitting here, with me talking for two. (Bright, brittle) Yes, some people contribute to the conversation; I pick up the check. Yes, someone SHOULD follow me around with a tape recorder—or a parrot! (To FRANK) And you, sitting there, smiling, basking in my neon nihilism, keeping up your little scrapbook of my insulting epigrams. (To jacket, as HE shakes it) I started to let you hang around! (To no one in particular, wandering, dragging jacket) Let, hell, I knew what I was doing. I knew what it took to keep you around—(To FRANK) And I put out. (To no one) Turning everything you said into a joke, giving you a little help with your ideas. (Southern accent) "Here, Jay; here's a little idea Ah had fo' a poem. Finish it in twenty-five words or less." (Screams) COLLABORATOR! And I did it! I gave myself to you. I did it, not you. I gave myself to you, and you didn't give one damned—(Takes jacket in his arms like a baby) . . . You gave your life, of course. (Suddenly, like one accused,

119

backing away from Ghost, from FRANK) But it wasn't worth anything to you without me—(To FRANK) And that IS based on actual experience! (To Ghost) So you loved me? So? How was I supposed to know it! You never said it! What was I supposed to do, go on producing indefinitely for you to keep on confiscating? (To FRANK) You crummy little Red, I don't WANT you here! (Spinning from Ghost to FRANK to jacket in his hands) You WANTED to give up your life, that's what you were here for, that's what you were DOING here, while I—

> HE stops, as if HE had never before considered this question, begins idly to pull on FRANK's jacket inside-out and backwards. It has a quilted silver lining. HE resembles Frankenstein's monster.

What WAS I doing? What was it. Day after night, pouring myself into—(HE looks down, rips the jacket off, throws it away. To jacket) Well, whatever I was doing—(To Ghost)—I used you to do it with—(To FRANK)—And I am not doing it anymore!

> (Goes to desk, opens drawer, takes out gun, walks immediately to FRANK, holds gun to FRANK's head) Get up.

> FRANK comes a little bit awake, looks into gun barrel, frowns, and goes back to sleep.

Get up.

> JAY shoots him in the head. It is, of course, a water gun. JAY drinks from it. FRANK shows no response at all. JAY lays gun down, goes over and takes a sip from some cold coffee—it is awful; HE gets an idea. HE takes the bottle of pills, opens them, shakes three of them into the coffee, stirs it with his finger, takes the boy's bag and loads it with a heavy stone or bricks used as bookends, replaces it, backs away from sofa, looks up to Ghost.

I'm sorry. (HE walks directly over to couch, gives it a resounding kick, and screams) GET UP! (FRANK stirs; chattily) I wonder if I should paint this place or just stay high all the time? (FRANK subsides, JAY repeats kick) GET UP!

FRANK: (Half-awake) What time is it?

JAY: The curtain was lowered to denote a lapse of memory. (As FRANK again subsides, aggressively) How'dja like my play?

FRANK: (Going to sleep) Great, great, great . . .

JAY: Great, great, grate on my nerves. (Leaps into the air and hops up and down on the sofa, shrieking) Get up! Get up! Get up up up up up!

FRANK: (Sits up) Hey!

JAY: (Sits innocently on back of sofa) Yes? What do you want?

FRANK: I don't want anything.

JAY: Gosh, it took me twentyseven years. (Pert) What do you want to do today?

FRANK: Sleep.

JAY: Okay, you've done that. Now have some coffee. (Offers it)

FRANK: I don't want any coffee.

JAY: Yes, you do; you said so when you came in. It's from last night. You'll never taste anything like it—till it comes up.

FRANK: I just want to sleep.

JAY: (Mock concern) Fight it, kid. Don't get hooked on it. I know! Have some black coffee! (Holds FRANK's nose, forces him to drink) Do you want a blindfold? That's right, drink it down like a little soldier.

FRANK: (Choking, sputtering) Okay, I drank it. Now I just want to sleep.

JAY: Not in about twenty minutes.

FRANK: Oh, my God. Why? Is somebody coming over?

JAY: (Terribly innocent) No, I put some Benzedrine spansules in your coffee.

FRANK: You WHAT?

JAY: (Speaking very clearly) I. Put. Benzedrine. Spansules. In. Your—

FRANK: My God!

JAY: No sugar.

FRANK: Benzedrine!

JAY: You looked so tired. I thought it would pep you up.
FRANK: That's a drug!
JAY: Like penicillin.
FRANK: People are allergic to drugs. I could die!

JAY: Don't be silly, there's not more than one chance in three.

FRANK: Christ, I need a shower. Don't you ever STOP?

JAY: No, if you stop, you think. (FRANK shows signs of settling back to sleep, so JAY attacks, "high-queen") Well, of course I stop! For a full moon, or a really good TV commercial, or a glass of coconut champagne in Times Square, or breakfast. What do you WANT for breakfast?

FRANK: I don't want any breakfast.

JAY: I've got this groovy new cereal in the shape of a jigsaw puzzle—

FRANK: Hey, don't; I can't take this this early—

JAY: You put it together, see—

FRANK: Please stop, okay?

JAY: —and it's an ad for the cereal. Sort of self-perpetuating, like the Village—"Each one teach one." (FRANK reaches for a cigarette; JAY snatches the pack) Isn't that terrible what they're making them put on cigarette packages? "CAUTION: Smoking can damage you health." Imagine if they made other products put on them what happens if you use too much, like—like—like Ajax, for instance. (Jimmy Durante voice) "Caution: use too much o'dis stuff, and yer hands'll look like a turkey's neck!" Or Doublemint. (Sings syrupy) "Chew double our gum and you'll bug out your eyes / And probably double your collar size!" Or—or—Vaseline! (Marlene Dietrich) "Careful, dollings, you can get too much of a good thing" Or they might hang a big sign at the entrance to Greenwich Village: "Beware: entering area of free expression; stagger around here too long and you're liable to get EXACTLY what you want!"

FRANK: (Numb) I realy need that shower—what are you ON?

JAY: Drugs? In the morning? How dare you? But I will take a few if it's necessary to make you feel better. (Pops a few) I guess that is how people get started—taking drugs to keep their junkie friends company. Oh, Frank, you really do need someone to take care of you. (Sudden succession of bright ideas) I need someone to take care of! I'll take care of you. You'll be taken care of by me! I'll be the one who takes care of you. You'll be the one care of whom I take! Oh, darling, you'll see, it'll be a lovely little life. All around the village they'll say, "Here come Frank and Jay!" No, I don't like that billing. Make it, "Here come Jay and Frank." (Coyly) Possibly, "Frank, care of Jay!" (Katherine Hepburn) Other people's lives, what are they? Debris, debris, piles of debris behind them. We'll make our lives a string of perfect disappearing days— starting with today. And I'll take you under my protecting thumb! I'll see that you get everything you want. What do you want, Frank? Tell me what you want and I'll give it to you.

FRANK: (Harassed to hysteria) I want a shower!

JAY: (Leaps into his arms) Darling! I'll give it to you!

FRANK: (Fights him off) Hey, come on, cut it out!

JAY: (Still doing "lost in a mist of romance") Listen— a shower sounds good. Think I'll go take one while there's still some hot water. And when I come back, we'll start our lovely new life with me reading you my novel! (Whisks out huge box of manuscript) You'll love it! It's based on the life of Lee Harvey Oswald. It's

123

very long, and very dull, but it perks up towards the end! Bye now—anything you need? (HE stands poised in the doorway)

FRANK: No! Go! Yes! Can I use your phone?

JAY: (Taking it out of wastebasket) Of course, silly. I can't use it in the shower, it's dangerous! Bye. (Grimly) Oh, and TELL Jo Wanda I said she can pay me later. She'll know what I mean. (Brightly) Ta-ta! See you real soon. (Starts off, returns) Oh, and Frank—if you WILL gobble that many pills at all hours of the day, you've got to watch out for hallucinaciones—seeing things? You can't tell what's real and what's not. (Starts walking out, but slows down like a dragging record) Whaat's reeal aand whaat's noot. Whaaaaat's reeeeeal aaaaaand whaaaaat's nooooot. (Starts to speed up, winds up sounding chipmunk) What's real and what's not Wh't's r'l 'nd w't's n't. Whtsrlndwhtsnt! (Skitters off, talking faster and faster till it is an electronic screech)

> FRANK, alone, does what any boy would do in the situation; HE bangs his head with his fists and screams silently. Then HE takes the phone and with mounting fury inwinds the cord from around it. HE dials—it seems to take hours—and then has to endure what seems to be the loudest phone-ring in history. Someone answers.

FRANK: Hello? John? . . . Oh, it's not John. What number have I . . . Okay, okay, I'm sorry. I mean, lo siento, Senora. Pardone mi, por favor.

> HE hangs up, gets a little slip of paper with John's phone number out of his pocket, drops it, has to scrabble among all the remnants of JAY's poem to find it, finds it, reseats himself, wearily dials again, waits, in the meantime examining the palm of his hand for hallucinations. You would think HE had never seen the palm of a hand before. John answers.

Hello! Jo Wanda? I mean John? Sorry to wake you, but . . . You just got up? What time is it? . . . Seven o'clock? My God, that play of his must have lasted for . . . No, never mind, I'll explain later, look, can I come over there? . . . Frank . . . FRANK! . . . Yeah, I'm still at his place, what did you think? . . . What do you mean, Old Faithful didn't blow last night? . . . Janice who?

We hear JAY offstage in the shower singing something like "Love Is Where You Find It," and gargling.

Oh, THAT Janice . . . Jesus. Look, can I come over there? . . . No, he's been swell . . . No, he hasn't ignored me . . . (Irate) No, he hasn't done that, either! I'll be right over . . . I'd like to shower there . . . I don't want to shower here . . . No, I told you he didn't! . . . All right, all right. I'll see you in a few minutes . . . Tell her what? . . . All right, please don't explain, I'll tell her—I mean HIM! . . . Okay. (Hangs up. HE now starts to get himself together, finding coat, dragging out bag, which is incredibly heavy, and putting it back, taking only his overnight bag. HE begins to hunt for his script, and in the process looks behind the sofa and pulls out Ed's picture, which seems to him, of course, to be his own—the last straw) Hey! (This is a cry of involuntary terror as HE drops picture back behind sofa)

JAY: (Off) Yes?

FRANK: Uh—I'm leaving! (Gets into coat, ties shoes)

JAY: (Off) Can't hear you. Be right out!

FRANK: I said I'm leaving! And I don't believe you about the hallucinations!

JAY: Just a minute! (HE enters, a-billow in an absurd, mind-blowing Mardi Gras outfit—fluorescent spangles and feathers, a flamingo fan, all topped off with a flowing Indian Chief's headdress. HE gets between FRANK and the door) Now, what was that about hallucinations?

FRANK: Uh—

JAY: You're not hallucinating, Frank; I really am wearing this two-piece bathing suit.

FRANK: Uh—I'm—going out.

JAY: Getting independent. That's a good sign in these cases. Remember, you can ask a policeman almost anything.

125

FRANK: (Shocked, drugged) Uh, yeah, Look—I can't handle my big
    bag right now. I'll—I'll come back for it.

JAY: Anytime. I work days.

FRANK: Uh—yeah, okay. (HE would love to get to the door) Oh, and
    Jo Wanda said to tell you she's going to—send something back
    with me?

JAY: (Grim) I'll bet she will. (Flirtatious, dredging key out of some
    deep pocket) Hey, look, I dug out my extra keys for you!

FRANK: (Accepting keys from as great a distance as possible) Oh. Well,
    thanks.

JAY: (Heavy wink) We'll skip the usual deposit. (HE steps aside to let
    FRANK go, but feels a pang of guilt and stops him at the door)
    Uh—look—do you need any money?

FRANK: (Puzzled by the kindness) Oh. No. Thank you very much—

JAY: Look, have fun in New York—really.

FRANK: Thanks, I will—I'll—hey, what are you—Oh, shit—I'll see
    you—I guess—

        JAY blows him a kiss and FRANK leaves quickly. JAY is
        jubilant the moment the door closes.

JAY: Hooray! Ah's delivered! No more ghosts! This happy hunting
    ground is hereby declared off limits! (Locks the door) Ah's
    delivered! Ah's delivered! (To mirror) How do I look delivered?
    Oooof! (Takes off headdress) No more deliveries, please! (Runs to
    window to watch FRANK walk away) Lumber, lumber, lumber!
    (Finds FRANK's script in shutter) Oh, Lordy! (Drops it like a hot
    potato) A dance in honour of my delivery! (Does a little Indian
    dance, suddenly stops) Oops! Better be careful. My magic is
    workin' so well today I might make it rain! Not bad for a first try.
    (Picks up coffee to toast himself) To the celebrated ghost chaser!
    (Drinks. It is the doped coffee) Oh. dear! I wonder what's the
    antidote to counteract a Benzedrine? Oh, hell! Here's to greater
    consciousness! (Drains cup) A benny for your thoughts! (Looks at
    messy room) Look at this mess! I almost let that kid fuck up my

126

whole—(HE is picking up poems when HE notices a special one)
Oh. I haven't even thought of this one for—(HE becomes
sentimental, goes to window to read poem by the morning
sunlight) "The hateful morning sun / interrupts a nightmare / of
my loved one." (Smiles sadly, shakes his head) "Nightmare of my
loved one." (To Ghost) What I actually dreamed was that you
were riding on a Ferris wheel with one of those battleship-class
weightlifter boyfriends of yours, and I was having to turn the
damned thing. (Ghost objects) Oh, all right, truck drivers. I can't
see that there's any great—(Realizes HE is talking to Ghost again)
Hey, what is this! I thought I just got rid of you for good! God
damn! You keep comin' back like a song, don'tcha?

SCENE 3

> The lights come up almost immediately. JAY, in black
> turtleneck and slacks, is preparing for FRANK's return. HE
> brings out fresh coffee, not bothering to clear the debris from
> Scene 2, talks to Ghost while doing so.

JAY: I am not talking to you. No, it will do you no good to moan, I am
not listening. I'll talk to you later, when I talk to him. Of course
he's coming back. You all come back! (HE holds up FRANK's
script to silence Ghost's arguments, seats himself, holding the
script)

> FRANK appears in the hallway. HE is dressed in Village
> clothes and looks rather stunning. HE starts to knock, then
> takes out his keys and opens the door. JAY, the moment he
> hears the keys rattle, tucks the script under a sofa cushion
> and assumes a bright, Loretta Young air. FRANK hesitates a
> moment more to run a comb through his hair, puffs up his
> chest, and enters.

FRANK: Hello. (Goes at once to his bag)

JAY: Hello. Coffee?

FRANK: (Taking bricks out of his bag) No thanks. What's in this batch,
Mescaline?

JAY: Novocaine.

127

FRANK: You sure drink an awful lot of coffee.

JAY: It keeps me wide awake. Sure you don't want some first?

FRANK: First before what? (HE begins to look around for his script)

JAY: Before we start fighting.

FRANK: What do you mean, "fighting?"

JAY: Well, you've been over to Jo Wanda's, and she gave you the real lowdown on me, and what a terrible phony I am, and you've come back here dressed to kill, so I naturally assumed it's me you're going to—

FRANK: (Interrupting) You know, you're a real bore.

JAY: Okay, we can start anywhere. Why am I a bore?

FRANK: You know, you're not worth talkin' to.

JAY: So? I do all the talking.

FRANK: You know, you're in love with yourself.

JAY: Jealous?

FRANK: The only thing I'm jealous about of you is your talent. I hate to see talent wasted.

JAY: When you could have used it?

FRANK: I told you, I'm a good writer.

JAY: (Runs to telephone) Sure, let's call your English teacher to prove it; I'm sure he'll accept the charges.

FRANK: (Grabs phone from JAY) What are you trying to do?

JAY: (Quick queen) How sweet. You noticed.

FRANK: You know, I feel sorry for you.

JAY: (Parodying the boy's hand-whacking gesture, right in FRANK's face) Honestly?

FRANK: You make me furious!

JAY: It works!

FRANK: What works?

JAY: Jiu-jitsu; using the other fellow's weight against him.

FRANK: I don't know what you're talking about.

JAY: That's all right. As you keep saying I keep saying, "I know."

FRANK: You know, I don't know which is worse; to know so much you can't learn any more, or to know so little you can't be taught!

JAY: Aha! You're falling into my style, I notice.

FRANK: Well, it's a good style; somebody ought to do something with it.

JAY: Like help the younger writers? Like get them in backstage? Like have them over to his house nights?

FRANK: Well, why not? If you won't help yourself, why not?

JAY: Not "Why not," baby, "Why?"

FRANK: Yeah, well, John told me that, too. Why you were so nice to me.

JAY: Well, come on, baby; bring in that surprise witness.

FRANK: (Brings Ghost's photo out) I look like that guy that died!

JAY: True, baby, you do. You look so much alike that you could have looked at each other and combed your hair. And combed your hair. And—

FRANK: You weren't even interested in me. All you wanted was my body.

JAY: And all you wanted was my mind.

FRANK: What if I did? What do you do with it but sit around here feeling sorry for yourself?

JAY: Instead of feeling sorry for whom?

FRANK: For that poor guy that killed himself—when you dropped him!

JAY: And others like him?

FRANK: I don't think you're capable of feeling anything for anybody!

JAY: Ho, boy! That's what our theater needs, brutal realism! Depraved queers and simple country boys! (Takes FRANK's script out, throws it at him) Come on, baby, read me THAT script!

FRANK: (Clutching the script) It's your SCRIPT. You're the one that always wants to turn everything into some kind of play. All I wanted was a little advice—

JAY: A little ventriloquism!

FRANK: Listen, we're both very bright. I thought we could pull it off together!

JAY: You mean watch each other masturbate?

FRANK: You're just trying to pick a fight!

JAY: I'm the perfect host. You came back for a fight.

FRANK: I came back for my bag and my script. I didn't want to see you again.

JAY: You've got a key. How come you came back when you knew I'd be here?

FRANK: You always win.

JAY: Only because I know it's a game.

FRANK: I don't know that game.

JAY: Oh, you play it awfully well, baby. You come in here with a smile and a song and a little wet dream of a play, and look up to me like the ghost of your English teacher, and I'm supposed to take it from there and go into the shadow-play that haunts this house! Only not this time. The position is filled. I've got a ghost of my own that fills all my needs.

FRANK: Ha! All except one. (HE slumps sexually)

JAY: Sorry. You can't afford me!

FRANK: You're disgusting.

JAY: All right, let's evade it. It's not the point, but let's evade it.

FRANK: How can you stand being—

JAY: (Mimicking "Whack" gesture) But evade it honestly!

FRANK: I hate to see a guy—

JAY: Truthfully!

FRANK: I could help you—

JAY: Fearlessly!

FRANK: All right! All right! You could help me! Is that what you want to hear me say? That I need you? I need you!

JAY: (Stunned, confused) You never go ahead and say the next thing. (Shakes it off) But that's all right. I don't want to hear it anymore. Jesus, how can even this be worse than I thought?

FRANK: What next thing? What did you say?

JAY: I said, "I'm going out the window. Do you want anything?"

FRANK: Out the—

JAY: It's the only thing open this late!

HE makes a sudden move as if to jump. FRANK leaps across
131   the room, grabs him, throws him down to the floor, slams the
window.

FRANK: You're crazy!

JAY: And you want me to stay that way! You want me to do it all over again! Jay, the mad scientist! You want me to praise you and pour myself into you and write your plays for you. You want me to take my brain out and put it into your body and make a ghost out of you and a corpse out of myself!

FRANK: That's insanity!

JAY: I call it death!

FRANK: Is this how you killed him?

JAY: He killed himself!

FRANK: Why?

JAY: From debt, baby, most suicides are from debt, and he owed me his soul!

FRANK: For what? Why? How come? What is this with you? What is this constant attitude that the world owes you something, that it's done you so wrong? What has it done to you? What has it done you out of? How did it do you in? What did it do to you? What did I do to you? What did he do to you that he owed you his soul? (Pause. Same volume) Huh?

JAY: Huh? Because it was my soul, that I had pumped into him, all the soul he ever had! And he never gave it back, soul or body, nothing, nothing, nothing!

FRANK: Well, did you ever come right out and ask for it back?

JAY: Why should I? He never had to ask me!

FRANK: Well, great! Cool! Fabulous! He didn't ask you for anything. You didn't ask him for anything. You didn't even ask him if he wanted WHATEVER it was you gave him! Why should you expect anything back, body, soul, whatever?

JAY: Because—I didn't want to make him into a monster. I didn't want to make him into a thief. I didn't want to make him into a ghoul.

132

But I didn't want him to make me into a grave-robber. I didn't want him to make me into a zombie. I didn't want him to make me into a comic-book devil, extracting souls from his helpless victims. I didn't want us to be Dr. Frankenstein and Charlie McCarthy. I wanted us to be beautiful. And instead, all I made of my quote mind and his quote body was just the usual ever-popular, show-stopping, handsome, toothsome, winsome and then some All-American hustler, Dead Ed. Baby, take a bow! ("Baby, take a bow!" directed to Ghost).

FRANK: Don't call me "baby!"

JAY: Why not? You applied for the role!

FRANK: I didn't apply for any "role." (Indicates scattered papers) I just helped you get rid of him.

JAY: Sure, that's what I created you for!

FRANK: It was YOU who wanted to audition me for some "role" or other—some kind of lover!

JAY: You want to be a paid substitute for a lover. What IS that word?

FRANK: You're out of your head!

JAY: YOU'RE out of my head!

FRANK: You just turn everything I say around!

JAY: Why? What have you been saying around?

FRANK: You just turn around everything I say!

JAY: Well, everything you say turns around me!

FRANK: You reverse everything I say!

JAY: Ya notice it makes just as much sense that way?

FRANK: Look, you don't want me!

JAY: You flatter me!

133

FRANK: You don't!

JAY: I never said I did.

FRANK: You don't want me and I don't want you. It's just some kind
of crazy defence you throw up when you think you're being
encroached upon. You come on and then you run away, again and
again!

JAY: (Simultaneously with FRANK's speech above) You keep digging
up your dull damned body and throwing it into the conversation
just when we're about to get somewhere important. And I want
you to STOP IT!

FRANK: You don't really want me and you know you don't. Hell, if I
grabbed you, you'd run!

JAY: (Outraged) Try it!

> FRANK hesitates for a moment and then grabs JAY in a
> clumsy embrace. JAY slaps him, hard.

(Waving his hand) Ouch! (To Ghost) Don't you people ever shave?

FRANK: (To Ghost, to JAY's great surprise) And you keep out of this!
(To JAY) You see? Neither of us wants this kind of relationship.

JAY: Not with you, we don't!

FRANK: You won't be serious!

JAY: All right, what do we want then? Tell us!

FRANK: I only wanted to be your friend!

JAY: My ghost!

FRANK: I didn't even know about the guy!

JAY: Weren't you counting on my devotion to some ghost of hopeless
love?

FRANK: Well, what if I was? What if you were to help me a little?

What if I was to let you? Wouldn't we both be getting what we want?

JAY: No! The ghost of it! The appearance of it! The feeling—just the imitation of the feeling. And we'd both have to give up our lives to get it. I'd tell you your dream, and you'd tell me mine, just so you could have the illusion of being respected, and I the illusion of being—

FRANK: I DO respect you!

JAY: —desired. Oh, God, suicide for that. And it is suicide, it is. You don't have to go as far as Ed did. The minute you try to live someone else's life for him, or let him live yours—it's suicide. And that's what we both wanted: to give up our lives to each other so we wouldn't have to live them ourselves. Say it with me. Say it. If I have to say it, at least say it with me. Because it's the honest truth for both of us: "I never wanted to buy you; I wanted to BE you."

FRANK: (Shaking his head) I better go. Jesus.

JAY: You might as well. We can't hurt each other anymore. Besides, we've got it all in our heads now—the last act, to play back at convenience. The un-original soundtrack.

FRANK: (At door) No. NO! What you're saying, all this mad scientist stuff, that witches' brew of mythology and psychology and Movie Mirror magazine in your head; I'll never think like that. Not unless I go crazy, too. (HE has meant this as an insult, but it brings a sudden realization) But then, that's true, isn't it? If I ever do start to go crazy, that way—I'll know it, won't I? Because I'll hear—your voice—in my head—saying all these things.

JAY: Like a ghost.

FRANK: No. Like a friend. Warning me. Thank you.

JAY: (Shocked, but guarded) So. You got a little piece of my mind after all. Well, I guess it's customary to give you boys SOMETHING. Goodbye. Tell Jo Wanda I'm sending back her "dish."

FRANK: Goodbye—(HE starts out, stops) Look—

135

JAY: Huh?

FRANK: You—gave me something that I needed very much.

JAY: Don't rub it in. (HE starts picking up Ed's papers, carefully)

FRANK: Look, you're living in the past.

JAY: (Bitterly) Have you got a present for me?

FRANK: You're so damned hard! I'd like to see you break, I really
would!

JAY: You and who else?

FRANK: I could break you!

JAY: Could you now?

FRANK: Yes, I could!

JAY: (Quietly) Honestly, truthfully, fearlessly?

FRANK: Yes. (HE thinks for a second) I love you. (HE exits)

> JAY stands staring at the door, then looks slowly around the
> room. The Ghost is gone; HE cannot find Ed anywhere. The
> phone rings. Not answering, JAY has the conversation HE
> knows he is going to have, in between phone rings.

JAY: Hello, Jo Wanda. (Ring) No, he's not. (Ring) Yes, he was. (Ring)
Yes, he has. (Ring) No, he won't be. (Answers phone) Hello? . . .
Oh, hello, Jo Wanda . . . No, he's not . . . Yes, he was . . . Yes, he
has . . . No, he won't be . . . Mad? Why should I be mad? . . . Oh,
that. Forget it . . . How DO I feel? . . . Oh, happy. Sleepy.
Grumpy. Bashful. Sneezy. Dopey. And Doc!

> HE slams the phone down, throws Ed's papers into waste-
> basket, and exits, dusting off his hands.

NOTES ON AUTHORS

LAURENCE COLLINSON

Although born in Leeds (1925) Laurence Collinson has spent most of his life in Australia and regards himself as an antipodean writer, even though expatriate. He is the author of two collections of poetry, many short stories, and a novel 'CUPID'S CRESCENT'. His plays for radio, television and the stage include 'THE ZALDA TRIO', a full-length stage play awarded a prize by The Elizabethan Theatre Trust and revived twice last year by London fringe theatres; a television script entitled 'THE CHEERFUL LANDLADY', which received a prize from the Society of Australian Authors; 'THE MOODS OF LOVE', a thirty-minute experimental verse play for Australian television; 'THE SLOB ON FRIDAY', an hour play for Canadian radio; and three plays for British Television: 'NUMBER THIRTY APPROXIMATELY', 'LOVING ISRAEL', and 'THE GIRL UPSTAIRS'. He contributes to Gay News and writes a regular column for the gay periodical 'Quorum'. In 1975 he was working on a second novel with a grant from the Literature Board of The Australian Council for the Arts. His main interest, apart from creative writing and gay liberation, is in the 'human potential movement', particularly in the fields of Transactional Analysis and Gestalt Therapy.

ROBERT PATRICK

Robert Patrick was born September 27, 1937, in the shadow of somebody else's oil well in Kilgore, Texas. His childhood was spent ostensibly in many different Depression states, but actually he grew up in the world-wide media mesh of slick-paper magazines, radio serials, paperback pocket books and above all before the slowly expanding screens of all-powerful Hollywood. This led him to New York, where, in 1961, he followed a Salvation Army Band to the Caffe Cino. He more or less lived there until it closed in 1968, proceeding to become, meanwhile, Off-Off Broadway's most-produced playwright with productions at the Cino, La MaMa, Playwright's Workshop, Gallery Theatre, Arts-East, Playbox Studio, and especially Norman "Speedy" Hartman's Old Reliable Theatre Tavern, Inc. His occasional plays for holidays hold a particular place in Off-Off Broadway history, and 'JOYCE DYNEL', his Old Reliable Easter show, won the Show Business Award as Best Off-Off Broadway Play of 1968-69.

His Off-Broadway productions include 'THE HAUNTED HOST' and 'CAMERA OBSCURA', which opened at the Cino, was subsequently included in 'COLLISION COURSE', and has since become a standard of both the professional and amateur repertory in America, Canada, England, and as far afield as Ceylon. It also popped up on National Education Television with Marge Champion, one of Mr. Patrick's idols.

His work has appeared in numerous anthologies, and in such magazines as 'yale/theatre', 'Intermission', 'Off-Off' and 'Astrology Today', and has been translated into German, Spanish and French. He originated the Edinburgh Festival's 'DRACULA', and has served as assistant director for Jerome Savary's Magic Circus and for Tom O'Horgan.

His play 'KENNEDY'S CHILDREN' received first prize in the Glasgow Citizen's Theatre World Playwriting contest in 1974 before opening at the King's Head Theatre in early 1975 (where it broke all records), and later transferring to the Arts Theatre, London.

Mr. Patrick resides on New York's Lower East Side, and his favorite authors are Ayn Rand, Herman Wouk, Jean Kerr, Shakespeare, Shaw and a number of others who would rather not be mentioned.

ALAN WAKEMAN writes:—

"I began writing for the theatre at the age of 8. Unfortunately, although my early plays for marionettes were received rapturously by the assembled children of the neighbourhood and were probably the best works of literature I will ever produce, they were never written down and are lost to posterity. Since then it has been downhill all the way. Novels and plays, poems and short stories have followed one another in bewildering profusion—most of them bad, all of them, mercifully, unpublished. By 1967 I had sunk so low as to publish an English language book for foreign students ('ENGLISH FAST', Hart-Davis Educational). Another 11 books on the same subject followed and worse was to come. In 1969 I published a book of photographs ('LONDONER'S LONDON', Rapp & Whiting) and by 1970 was even writing articles for learned journals such as Visual Education and the Journal of English Teaching, and broadcasting talks on the B.B.C. (with titles like 'Administrative Problems of Classroom Tape Recorders'). I also managed to waste a lot of time studying architecture for four years, painting houses in Paris, waiting tables on the Ile du Levant, nursing radio transmitters in Ceylon, driving taxis in London, designing schools in Japan—well, you get the picture. Lately though I would like to think there has been an improvement. Last year I published a distinctly frivolous card game called 'JABBERWOCKY' (Longman, 1974) and this autumn I have a book coming out called 'TIM, WILLIE & THE WURGLES' (Abelard-Schuman, 1975). I leave it to the reader to decide where 'SHIPS' fits into this strange mosaic. I would like to record my thanks here, to the cast of the original production for their many suggestions, most of which I managed to ignore, but a few of which they contrived to sneak in despite me, thereby contributing to the play's virtues and obliging me to admit grudgingly that they were right. For the play's faults I am, of course, completely responsible."

ED BERMAN

In 1968, this expatriate American founded Inter-Action Trust and now works as the Artistic Director of Inter-Action Productions (including The Ambiance Lunch-Hour Theatre Club, The Almost Free Theatre, the Fun Art Bus and the Dogg's Troupe). As ED.B., he has written six plays produced in London including 'SAGITTARIUS', 'VIRGO' and 'THE NUDIST CAMPERS GROW AND GROW'.

For the Ambiance, he has directed several plays including the premieres of John Arden's 'SQUIRE JONATHAN', 'THE WINDOW' by Frank Marcus, James Saunder's 'DOG ACCIDENT' and 'SAVOURY MERINGUE', and Tom Stoppard's 'DOGG'S OUR PET'. Like other members of Inter-Action's co-operative, he divides his time between the production company and work in schools, youth clubs, mental hospitals, community centres, playgrounds, remand homes and the streets.

Most of his time is now spent in creating new community arts and action projects on behalf of Inter-Action, such as City Farm 1: The Fun Art Farm. He still manages to direct some 10 plays a year mainly for children's and community theatre and performs in 200 odd shows a year. Prof. R.L. Dogg (a pseudonym) writes verse for children.

In real life he is the head of the Father Xmas Trade Union, Chairman of the Save Piccadilly Campaign, Chairman of the National Association of Arts Centres and Hon. Treasurer of the Fair Play for Children Campaign.

ABOUT INTER-ACTION

Inter-Action is a charitable trust founded in 1968 by Ed Berman to stimulate community involvement in the arts, especially through the use of drama and creative play, and to experiment in theatre/media and their social applications.

The work of Inter-Action is broadly divided into two categories— theatre and community work. In addition to The Almost Free Theatre activities, Inter-Action Productions embraces the work of the Dogg's Troupe, O.A.T.S. (Old Age Theatre Society), Infilms and the Fun Art Bus. All activities are administered by a co-operative of artists and community workers whose time is shared between the production company and work done in schools, youth clubs, mental hospitals, community centres, playgrounds, remand homes and the streets.

The Ambiance Lunch-Hour Theatre Club at The Almost Free Theatre is a showcase for premiere productions of one-act plays. It provides a vehicle for young and established actors, writers and directors to try new ideas without financial pressures. The Ambiance is open to ideas from everyone. Since there is no permanent Ambiance company of actors, casts are newly formed for every play. Associate Directors include Clive Barker, Jack Emery, Pedr James, Roland Rees, Geoffrey Reeves, Anton Rodgers, Prunella Scales and Tom Stoppard.

Evenings At The Almost Free was formerly a showcase time for Inter-Action's The Other Company. With the tragic death of its brilliant director, Naftali Yavin, the company has ceased operation. Since 1973, evening productions have pursued a similar policy to the Ambiance but for full-length plays and projects.

The community work side of the trust has fifty members who live and work co-operatively in Kentish Town, London Borough of Camden. The work is varied, ranging from a new community arts resource centre to a three-acre farm in the middle of London (renovated out of a derelict timber yard) with stables and an indoor riding school. (City Farm 1: Inter-Action's Fun Art Farm).

Other aspects of Inter-Action's community work include an Advisory Service for self-help groups, the Community Media Van, a studio-on-wheels for community action, the Training Unit which specialises in the Inter-Action Game Method, a community play programme and a

141

project for school refusers sponsored by the Inner London Education
Authority.

The skills, training and prestige of the theatre side of the work are
applied to an innovatory approach in the use of communications for
community work. In 1970, a Council of Europe report described
Inter-Action as "the most exciting community arts project in
Europe . . . Inter-Action is praised by almost everyone—from both
inside and outside the establishment."